# The Sufi Science
of Self-Realization

# The Sufi Science of Self-Realization

A Guide to
the Seventeen Ruinous Traits,
the Ten Steps to Discipleship
and
the Six Realities of the Heart

Shaykh Muhammad Hisham Kabbani

Foreword by
Shaykh Muhammad Nazim Adil al-Haqqani

FONS VITAE

First published in 2006 by
FonsVitae
49 Mockingbird Valley Drive
Louisville, KY 40207
http://www.fonsvitae.com

Copyright Fons Vitae 2006

Library of Congress Control Number: 2006921245

ISBN 1-930409-29-X

Published in association with
the Institute for Spiritual and Cultural Advancement.

Printed in Canada.

Library of Congress Cataloging-in-Publication Data

Kabbani, Shaykh Muhammad Hisham.
        The Sufi science of self-realization: a guide to the seventeen
ruinous traits, the ten steps to discipleship, and the six realities of
the heart / by Shaykh Muhammad Hisham Kabbani.
        p. cm.
ISBN 1-930409-29-X1.
Sufism. 2. Self realization—Religious aspects—Islam. 3.Asceticism—
Islam. 4. Religious life—Islam. I. Title.
        BP189.6.K24 2005
        297.4'4—dc22

# CONTENTS

## PUBLISHER'S NOTES

This book is specifically designed for laypersons and readers unfamiliar with Sufi terms. As such, we have often replaced Arabic terminology with English translations, except in instances where Arabic terms are crucial to the tone and substance of the text. In such instances, we have included transliterations or footnoted explanations.

As the source material is an oral transmission, its language was revised for a written format, and references have been added as appropriate; however, we have tried our best to retain the essence of the author's original talks. We ask the reader's forgiveness for any omissions in this final text.

For those who are familiar with Arabic and Islamic teachings, we apologize for the simplified transliterations. Our experience is that unfamiliar symbols and diacritical marks make for difficult reading by laypersons; as such, please indulge this compromise between accuracy and accessibility.

Qur'anic quotes are centered, highlighted in italics and footnoted, citing chapter name, number and verse. The Holy Traditions of Prophet Muhammad ﷺ (known as Prophetic Tradition) are offset, italicized and footnoted referencing the book(s) in which they are cited, while extensive explanations or commentary are placed in endnotes.

Where gender-specific pronouns such as "he" and "him" are applied in a general sense, it has been solely for the flow of text, and no discrimination is intended towards female readers.

## Universally Recognized Symbols

The following Arabic symbols connote sacredness and are universally recognized by Sufi Muslims:

The symbol ﷾ represents *subhanahu wa ta'ala,* a high form of praise reserved for God alone, which is customarily recited after reading or pronouncing the common name Allah, and any of the ninety-nine Islamic Holy Names of God.

The symbol ﷺ represents *sall-Allahu 'alayhi wa sallam* (God's blessings and greetings of peace be upon the Prophet), which is customarily recited after reading or pronouncing the holy name of Prophet Muhammad ﷺ.

The symbol ﷵ represents *'alayhi 's-salam* (peace be upon him/her), which is customarily recited after reading or pronouncing the sanctified names of prophets, Prophet Muhammad's ﷺ family members, and the angels.

The symbol ﵁ / ﵂ represents *radi-allahu 'anh/'anha* (may God be pleased with him/her), which is customarily recited after reading or pronouncing the holy names of Prophet Muhammad's ﷺ Companions.

The symbol ق represents *qaddas-allahu sirrah* (may God sanctify his or her secret), which is customarily recited after reading or pronouncing the name of a saint.

The honorific *Sayyidina/Sayyida* (our master/our lady), precedes the names of prophets, Companions and Sufi saints and masters.

Shaykh Muhammad Nazim ʿAdil al-Qubrusi

# ABOUT THE AUTHOR

Shaykh Muhammad Hisham Kabbani is a world-renowned author and religious scholar. He has devoted his life to the promotion of the traditional Islamic principles of peace, tolerance, love, compassion and brotherhood, while opposing extremism in all its forms. The shaykh is a member of a respected family of traditional Islamic scholars, which includes the former head of the Association of Muslim Scholars of Lebanon and the present Grand Mufti[1] of Lebanon.

In the U.S., Shaykh Kabbani serves as Chairman, Islamic Supreme Council of America; Founder, Naqshbandi-Haqqani Sufi Order of America; Advisor, World Organization for Resource Development and Education; Chairman, As-Sunnah Foundation of America; Chairman, Kamilat Muslim Women's Organization; and, Founder and President, The Muslim Magazine.

Shaykh Kabbani is highly trained, both as a Western scientist and as a classical Islamic scholar. He received a bachelor's degree in chemistry and studied medicine. In addition, he also holds a degree in Islamic Divine Law, and under the tutelage of Shaykh 'Abd Allah Daghestani ق, license to teach, guide and counsel religious students in Islamic spirituality from Shaykh Muhammad Nazim 'Adil al-Qubrusi al-Haqqani an-Naqshbandi ق, the world leader of the Naqshbandi-Haqqani Sufi Order.

His books include: *Pearls and Coral* (2005); *Keys to the Divine Kingdom* (2005); *Classical Islam and the Naqshbandi Sufi Order* (2004);

---

[1] The highest Islamic religious authority in the country.

*The Naqshbandi Sufi Tradition Guidebook* (2004); *The Approach of Armageddon? An Islamic Perspective* (2003); *Encyclopedia of Muhammad's Women Companions and the Traditions They Related* (1998, with Dr. Laleh Bakhtiar); *Encyclopedia of Islamic Doctrine* (7 vols. 1998); *Angels Unveiled* (1996); *The Naqshbandi Sufi Way* (1995); *Remembrance of God Liturgy of the Sufi Naqshbandi Masters* (1994).

In his long-standing endeavor to promote better understanding of classical Islam, Shaykh Kabbani has hosted two international conferences in the United States, both of which drew scholars from throughout the Muslim world. As a resounding voice for traditional Islam, his counsel is sought by journalists, academics and government leaders.

Shaykh Muhammad Hisham Kabbani
with Shaykh Muhammad Nazim.

# PREFACE
## ON THE SUFI SCIENCE OF SELF-REALIZATION

*We shall show them Our Signs on the horizons and*
*within themselves until it will be manifest unto them*
*that it is the Truth.*[2]

T he use of the word "science" in the title of this collection is perfectly appropriate, as science pertains to knowledge, but it is only modern science that has developed knowledge at the expense of the human soul. This is remarkable because the foundations of modern science rest upon an understanding of the interrelatedness of the soul and the world. The icon of modern science, Sir Isaac Newton, was a devoted student of alchemy, a traditional science concerned above all with the correspondence between the world, or macrocosm, and the human microcosm. Indeed, all traditional sciences depend upon this relationship.

Shaykh Muhammad Hisham Kabbani, a teacher educated in both the traditional and modern sciences, begins this collection with the insight that "everything in this world has significance to the lives of human beings." Self-knowledge is inseparable from the history of science, even if modern science prefers to deny it.

The Sufi Science of Self-Realization arrives in an age of unrivalled scientific manipulation of the material aspect of existence. As if to balance these material developments, the teachings presented here outline a course toward spiritual

---

[2] Surah Fussilat [Clearly Spelled Out], 41:53.

realization that has never before been made available *en masse*. In this book, he reveals that technology itself "imitates the abilities of spiritual teachers."

Every science is formulated in terms of number. The science presented here is no different, with its three sections containing specific numbers of elements. It is precisely in regard to numbers that a distinction may be perceived between the modern and traditional sciences. Whereas modern science uses numbers solely in their quantitative aspects, traditional sciences proceed on the basis of a qualitative understanding of numbers, that is, their meaning for the human soul. This traditional understanding is perhaps best termed Pythagorean, since the qualitative significance of number dominated the perspective of this Classical doctrine. When Islamic writings developing this perspective appeared in the context of the medieval awakening of European science, their universal validity was easily recognized by other religious communities. For example, it is known that the *Book of Circles* by the Spanish Muslim Ibn Sid was translated by Jewish scholars and was also among the influences on the Christian Ramon Lull, whose "machine" of circles has been recognized as prefiguring the computer.

Among the numbers specific to The Sufi Science of Self-Realization, seventeen appears in a negative context that contrasts with its historically positive significance. In the traditions of Islam, seventeen figures as the original number of knights invested as masters of chivalry. For this reason, it may be mentioned that seventeen lights are borne in the Grail procession as described in the masterwork of medieval Christian chivalry, *Parzival*, by Wolfram von Eschenbach. More importantly, seventeen is the most significant number in the teachings of Jabir Ibn Hayyan, the alchemist known to Christendom as Geber the Arabian Prince. It is of interest to note that the spiritual master of Jabir Ibn Hayyan was Imam Ja'far as-Sadiq, who is included in the Golden Chain of Masters of the Naqshbandi Order from which Shaykh Muhammad Hisham Kabbani derives his authority. In his writings on "Balance," Jabir maintains that seventeen is the key to understanding the structure of the world. His writings constitute an application of a "Science of Letters" related to the science of numbers, since each letter of the Arabic alphabet has a numeric value; such a perspective also exists in relation to the Greek and Hebrew alphabets.

The number ten figures prominently in this work, as indeed it did for the Greek Pythagoreans. The same may be observed for the Hebrew Qabbalists, according to whom there are ten Sephiroth. It should likewise be observed that the Hebrew root of the word "Qabbala" has more than a casual relationship with the Arabic word "Qiblah," a term explained by the shaykh at the beginning of his discussion of the "Ten Steps." Ten is also the most significant number in the aforementioned *Book of Circles* by Ibn Sid.

The significance of the number six for the Pythagoreans was such that the Great Shaykh of Sufism, Ibn al-'Arabi, mentioned them in his writings specifically in connection with this number. Shaykh Kabbani describes the six powers of the heart as hidden by a black spot. Clearly, this is the black spot of the heart mentioned by Ibn al-'Arabi some eight centuries ago. In translating his descriptive term for this black spot, Annemarie Schimmel and others have chosen the alchemical term "Philosopher's Stone," not so much for its literal equivalence, but rather for its marvelous and transformative implications. Half a millennium after Ibn al-'Arabi, the Naqshbandi Shah Wali Allah of India, reintroduced this "Philosopher's Stone" in his description of the Subtle Points (*lata'if*) of the human form. However, only in this work has such a full treatment of this mystery been presented. It is worth remembering that, among the alchemists of Europe, the Philosopher's Stone was symbolized by the intersecting triangles of the six-pointed star—a geometric representation of the number six. Such remarkable accord is no doubt a confirmation of the reality of this science.

In the verse of the Qur'an referred to above, (Surah Fussilat, 41:53) the word for "sign" (*ayah*) in its macrocosmic ("on the horizons") and microcosmic ("within themselves") dimensions is also the name for "verse." Among the letters that form the verses of the Qur'an, there are three—*alif, waw* and *ya*—that have a special grammatical role.[3] Two of these, *ya* and *waw*, have the numerical values of ten and six respectively. According to the Science of Letters, the *ya* may symbolize corporeal existence while the *waw* may symbolize the angelic realm, and so the passage from the "Ten Steps" to the "Six Powers" may be understood to relate to this symbolism. The *alif*, with a numerical value of one, may symbolize the Divine Realm, and so the shaykh's mysterious concluding comment concerning an additional reality of the heart may complete a three-fold "sign" within the human being. Again, according to the Science of Letters and in particular the writings of Ibn al-'Arabi, these three letters also represent the highest office-holders in a spiritual government; and so Shaykh Kabbani's frequent references to high-level clearance in government work should not be taken too lightly.

To conclude these remarks, it may be observed that the sum of the numerical values of *alif, waw* and *ya* is seventeen. Not only does this calculation restore the number seventeen in this collection to its positive significance, but the negative characteristics perverting the soul may then be recognized as being a precise inversion of the spiritual government helping the soul in its quest for knowledge. The Science of the Balance, in which the number seventeen figures so prominently, provides an understanding of how the inner and outer aspects of a thing may be brought to perfection. The shaykh describes the person who attains "the inner and outer in harmony" as gold, to be understood in the highest alchemical sense. The Sufi Science of Self-Realization provides not only a reminder of the inner potential of the soul, but also the real possibility of restoring that

---

[3] Arabic characters are *alif* ا, *waw* و, and *ya* ي.

cosmic balance which has long been sought as both the Philosopher's Stone and Holy Grail. It should hardly be surprising, then, that it is Shaykh Muhammad Hisham Kabbani who has systematized to an unprecedented degree this possibility in a world which has lost its balance, for *"kabban"*[4] literally means an instrument for finding the balance of things.

Mahmoud Shelton
April 21, 2005
Ashland, Oregon

---

[4] Arabic. *qabban.*

The Station of Extinction, *Maqam al-Fana*, is one of the primary stations on the Path of the Sufi towards the State of Perfection, *Maqam al-Ihsan*. This station in fact is the first target of the seeker as he moves on the way of spiritual wayfaring, and while not the ultimate final destination, its attainment is considered the first foothold into the Garden of Sainthood—for one who reaches this has become of the Elect. It is for this reason that many identified this station as the final goal and declared that one who attained it had in fact achieved ultimate felicity, complete nothingness. Whereas in reality, this station, while of immense magnitude, is still a waystation on the ascent towards the Divine. For this reason the Naqshbandi Saints said, "Our Way begins where others leave off."

In the station of extinction, the servant of God leaves his very self behind, and in abandonment of all that pertains to selfhood is cut adrift in the oceanic realm of God's Reality. At that station, self-realization is achieved for the seeker has achieved the Vision of Witnessing, *'aynu 'l-mushahadah*, and is thus able to testify with true vision, as a witness of the One. When that is attained, the seeker is unable to identify him or herself as existent and sees all existence as a manifestation of the Oneness of God.

## THE CITY OF KNOWLEDGE

The Prophet Muhammad ﷺ, who was the leader of humanity in seeking the Divine Presence, said:

*I am the City of Knowledge and ʿAli is its gate.*[5]

In this statement is an affirmation of two realities:

- The Prophet ﷺ encompasses all knowledge granted to creation from the Lord of Creation.
- ʿAli ibn Abi Talib ؓ, the Lion of God, was chosen as the one through whom access to that knowledge was made possible.

As regards the first point, God said:

> *He discloses not His unseen (ghayb) to anyone, except only to such a Messenger as He is well-pleased with.*[6]

Muhammad ﷺ is the Crown of those messengers with whom God is well-pleased. As a prophet who brought reports from His Lord; as the one who ascended above the seven heavens and the seven Paradises to His Lord's Presence by *"two bows' length or even nearer"*[7]; as the one who told of the events that attended the creation of all existent beings; as the one who saw the events after resurrection and Judgment Day, and as the one to whom was revealed the inimitable Qur'an, who is more deserving of such a boundless gift—the gift of Knowledge from the Divine Presence? If about a saint, as our master Khidr عليه السلام is regarded by many scholars, (while others assert he was a prophet), about whom God said, *"We had taught knowledge from Our own Presence,"*[8] how would it not be befitting that the All-wise Creator grant the entire body of heavenly knowledge to His Beloved ﷺ. For the Lord of the heavens and the earth said of him:

> *And We granted you knowledge of what you knew not, and the bounty of Allah for you has been infinite.*[9]

And He, the Almighty said:

---

[5] Narrated by al-Hakim (*sahih*) and at-Tirmidhi (*hasan*).
[6] Suratu 'l-Jinn [The Jinn], 72:26.
[7] Suratu 'n-Najm [The Star], 53:9.
[8] Suratu 'l-Kahf [The Cave], 18:65.
[9] Suratu 'n-Nisa [Women], 4:113.

*This is of the tidings of the Unseen which we reveal to you. You did not know it before this, nor your people.*[10]

Also regarding the knowledge granted him by His Lord, the Prophet ﷺ said:

*My Lord came to me in the best image and asked me over what did the angels of the higher heaven vie, and I said I did not know, so He put His hand between my shoulders, and I felt its coolness in my innermost, and the knowledge of all things between the East and the West came to me.*[11] i

*In this regard, a man from Banu Amir, asked the Prophet ﷺ, "Is there any knowledge left which you do not know?" whereupon the Prophet ﷺ said, "God has taught me a great good, and there is a kind of Unseen knowledge which God alone knows..."*[12]

The statement *"I am the City of Knowledge and 'Ali is its gate"* means that Muhammad ﷺ was the essence of the heavens itself; the fabric of creation itself in its entirety. The evidence of this is the famous narration of Jabir ﷺ.

*Jabir ibn Abd Allah ﷺ said to the Prophet ﷺ, "O Messenger of God, may my father and mother be sacrificed for you, tell me of the first thing God created before all things." He said: "O Jabir, the first thing God created was the light of your Prophet from His light, and that light remained*[13] *in the midst of His Power for as long as He wished, and there was not, at that time, a Tablet or a Pen or a Paradise or a Fire or an angel or a heaven or an earth. And when God wished to create creation, he divided that Light into four parts and from the first made the Pen, from the second*

---

[10] Surah Hud, 11:49.
[11] Tirmidhi and Baghawi in *Sharh al-Sunnah*.
[12] Ahmad narrated it and Abu Dawud narrated part of it.
[13] Literally: "turned."

*the Tablet, from the third the Throne, then He divided the fourth into four parts [and from them created everything else]."*[14]

## THE LIGHT OF CREATION

The light of the First Creation was the Muhammadan Reality and from that Light all other creation came into existence. It was in truth the creation of Muhammad which is the reason for the existence of all things, as God said in a Holy Tradition[15]:

*If not for you [O Muhammad] I would not have created the cosmos.*[16]

All that is conveyed in the first verse revealed to the Prophet ﷺ, Iqra – *"Read!"*[17] for from its outwardly apparent meaning, *"Read in the name of thy Lord who created"*[18] the mention of the Lord's creation is first. This means, "I order you to read, O Muhammad, in My name, for I am the one Who created You, and from you all creation emerged."

God's Order for creation proceeded from the Divine Essence and resulted in the creation of the Muhammadan Reality, *al-Haqiqat al-Muhammadiyyah*. God is the One who caused it to emerge in the way that He liked. Thus the Prophet's light exists in everything for which God said:

*And know that within you is God's Messenger.*[19]

Gabriel ﷺ did not say, "Recite!" for recitation comes from what is already known and held in the mind, but reading refers to something that must first be seen in order to be read. If God was ordering Prophet Muhammad to read, it means before him was

---

[14] Abd ar-Razzaq in his *Musannaf*. Bayhaqi, with a different wording, in *Dalail al-nubuwwah* according to Zurqani in his *Sharh al-mawahib* and Diyarbakri in *Tarikh al-khamis*.

[15] Prophetic Tradition - *hadith qudsi*.

[16] al-Ajlouni, *Kashf al-Khafa*, Ali al-Qari, *Sharh al-Shifa*.

[17] Suratu 'l-'Alaq [The Clot], 96:1.

[18] *Ibid*.

[19] Suratu 'l-Hujarat [The Private Apartments], 49:7.

something which could be read – from it he was looking and reading. What was he reading? He was reading *"in the name of your Lord Who Created."* It means, "O Muhammad! I am granting and then opening to you knowledge of the secret of creation; the secret of which was never opened before."

Even today's scientists still do not know the secret of when the soul reaches the embryo in the womb of the mother. God gave that secret to Muhammad ﷺ when He said, "Read!" where it means, "See; for I am showing you, so read and learn, and know that in My Name I am showing you My Creation."

Creation of the universe is easy. But as God said, to create one human being is not easy. He said, *"Who created the human being from a clot."* That clot has been identified today by scientists as the female's egg fertilized by one sperm.

A woman normally produces one or two eggs at one time and at most eight. But the man gives forth 500 million sperm at one time. From that huge number God allows only one sperm to connect with the single egg. This secret and further secrets which have yet to be disclosed to humankind, were granted to the Prophet ﷺ in that first revelation.

When Gabriel ﷺ said "read!" the Prophet ﷺ was unlettered (*umiyyun*), he did not know how to handle a pen, yet God ordered him to "Read!" The secret of this comes in the second repetition of the order to "read!":

> *Read and your Lord is most Generous who taught*
> *humankind by means of the pen; taught humankind*
> *what it knew not.*[20]

It means, "Read in the name of thy Lord who taught You O Muhammad, the Original Man, by means of the Pen."

It was no ordinary pen that God mentioned to Prophet Muhammad ﷺ such as those carried by people today. *"Who taught humankind by means of the pen"* refers to the Pen of Power (*Qalam*

---

[20] Suratu 'l-'Alaq [The Clot], 96:3.

al-Qudrah), the Pen by which the Beautiful Names of God were inscribed on the Preserved Tablet (al-Lawh al-Mahfudh). It is the Pen that wrote the destinies of all created beings before God brought them from the world of possibilities into the world of existence. About it, the Prophet ﷺ said:

> God inscribed the destinies of all created things before creating the heavens and the earth by fifty thousand years, while His Throne stood upon the water.[21]

It is narrated:

> Before creating any of the cosmos God ordered the Pen to write, and it said, "What should I write?" and He said, "Write: there is no god except God (la ilaha ill-Allah.)" So for 70,000 years the Pen wrote la ilaha ill-Allah.
>
> And then God said again, "Write!" And the Pen asked, "What should I write?" He said, "Write Muhammad is the Prophet of God (Muhammadun Rasulullah.)"
>
> And so for 70,000 years the Pen wrote Muhammadun Rasulullah. The Pen asked, "Who is that Muhammad that you put his name with Your Name?" God said, "Silence! If not for Muhammad I would not have created creation."[ii]

Whatever God has created emerged from His Ocean of Power (bahr al-qudrah), and whatever exists in this universe is under the power and authority of Sayyidina Muhammad ﷺ and all of that is contained in the Muhammadan Reality. Now whereas the Muhammadan Reality is in fact the essence and source of all created beings, therefore within himself our master Muhammad ﷺ holds knowledge of all creation:

> Say: "If the ocean were ink (wherewith to write out) the
> words of my Lord, sooner would the ocean be exhausted
> than would the words of my Lord, even if we added
> another ocean like it, for its aid."[22]

---

[21] Sahih Muslim.
[22] Suratu 'l-Kahf [The Cave], 18:109.

And this is followed by a reference to the Prophet ﷺ himself, indicating that the Oceans of God's Knowledge described in the preceding verse are in fact in his possession, despite his tremendous humility and sense of non-existence before the Greatness of His Lord:

> Say: "I am but a man like yourselves, (but) the inspiration has come to me, that your God is only One God: whoever expects to meet his Lord, let him work righteousness, and, in the worship of his Lord, admit no one as partner."[23]

And as the Prophet ﷺ is the holder of the Oceans of Divine Knowledge, Sayyidina 'Ali ؛ is the bridge one crosses to ascertain that reality.

Thus those who seek to traverse in the Paths of God, must seek the means in our master, 'Ali ؛, and his teachings. Where are such teachings to be found? It is a truism that "he who seeks shall find," and thus the sincere seeker, immediately upon setting out with firm intention, will be guided to the Door of Knowledge and River of Truth which stems from the heart of Sayyidina 'Ali ؛ and the hearts of the other three rightly-guided caliphs of the Prophet ﷺ.

When the Prophet ﷺ described 'Ali ؛ as the Door of the City of Knowledge it means, "I am the one carrying the secrets that God has given to humanity because I am the one from whose light God created creation. I am but a servant, but He gave me that honor." So he ﷺ told our master 'Ali ؛, "Explain to them from those realities."

From these wisdoms we know that even the Companions, despite all their high levels of spiritual attainment, none of them could understand the reality of Sayyidina Muhammad ﷺ except two: Abu Bakr as-Siddiq ؛ and 'Ali ibn Abi Talib ؛. Sayyidina

---

[23] Suratu 'l-Kahf, 18:110.

'Ali ﷺ was given the task of explaining from these realities to the Companions. An example of that is:

> It is reported that when 'Umar ibn al-Khattab ﷺ performed pilgrimage and kissed the (Black) Stone, he said, "I know by God that you are a stone which neither harms nor benefits, and had I not seen God's Messenger kiss you, I would not have embraced you."
>
> However, 'Ali ibn Abi Talib ﷺ said to him, "Abu Hafs, do not say this, for God's Messenger ﷺ did not kiss it (the Black Stone) save for wisdom he knew: It has two eyes and two lips and possesses a keen tongue that testifies for those who fulfill their obligations to it."[24]

So in fact Sayyidina 'Ali ﷺ was explaining to Sayyidina 'Umar ﷺ, reminding him of the Prophetic Tradition which he had forgotten. Both the modern scholars (al-mutaqqadimin) and the scholars of old agree that whoever wants to understand the reality of eternal life must go through the heart of Sayyidina 'Ali ﷺ and the heart of the family of the Prophet ﷺ, for God told the Prophet ﷺ:

> Say, I ask of you no payment except love of my relatives.[25]

It means, "Love my near of kin in order to be granted from the Divine realities and secrets, for they are the vehicles of my light and carriers of my knowledge. They are the means by which to know that God has adorned me with on the Day of Promises."

While the door to Sayyidina Muhammad's ﷺ city is Sayyidina 'Ali ﷺ, and there is only one door, inside the city is what the Prophet ﷺ has given to the Veracious One, Abu Bakr as-Siddiq ﷺ. He is inside that city watching over the jewels that are within its most valued treasure chest. The Prophet ﷺ is the knowledge itself.

---

[24] Reported by Imam Ghazali, *Ihya 'ulum ad-din*, and, Hajjah Amina Adil, *Lore of Light*, volume 1, p.24, with additional wording.
[25] Suratu 'sh-Shura [Consultation], 42:23.

There is someone receiving and keeping that treasure and that is Sayyidina Abu Bakr as-Siddiq ☙.

## SAINTS IN HIDING

Speaking of the station of extinction, Sayyidina 'Ali ☙ said in verse:

*I saw my Lord with the eye of my heart*
*I said: No doubt it's You! It's You!*
*You are the One who encompassed every "where"*
*so that there is no "where," except You are there*
*"Where" has no "where" in regards to You*
*for "where" to know where You are*
*nor can imagination, imagine You*
*for imagination to know where You are*
*Your knowledge encompasses everything*
*so that everything I see is You*
*and in my annihilation, is the annihilation of my annihilation*
*and in my annihilation, I found You.*[26]

So when we see this kind of poetry and this kind of love, this description of the state of annihilation; when we see this kind of relationship between the human being and His Lord, where then is there room for human beings to spend on this worldly life? It is in that state of awe and non-existence that the Lovers and Friends of God find themselves. And when they are in this state, no one can approach them.

Al-Hasan ibn al-Mansour ق said:

The identity of God's elect servant, the Sufi, becomes extinguished in the Divine Presence. No one bears such a person nor does that person put up with [standards of behavior] others [tolerate]. Still, the elect one among God's servants is like unto the earth; it accepts every type of

---

[26] From *The Commentary of the Hikam of Ibn Ataillah as-Sakandari* by Ibn Ajiba. (*'Ikaz al-himmam fee sharhi al-hikam li Ahmad bin Muhammad bin Ajiba al-Hasani*).

refuse and yet nothing issues from it but sweetness. Both the good and the sinner walk over and step on the servant of God. And the vilest of creation are they who pretend to be the elect of God when in fact they are stingy.

Ash-Shibli ق said, "The Sufi is cut off from creatures and connected to the Truth."[27] Ibn Ajiba ق relates that it has been said, "Whoever possesses states whose character indicates proximity to God is insupportable. The mountains carry him not." Such is the aspect of whoever realizes the station of extinction, *Maqam al-fana*. Al-Hasan ibn al-Mansour ق wrote of the one who became extinguished (*fani*) in the love of God [28]:

People find it difficult to tolerate the one who has lost any sense of self and who stands in awe, stunned before God's Absolute Existence. Whoever reaches that station (*maqam*) and would in any way divulge its secret, will act differently from the commonality of humankind.

For that reason, the Friends of God (*awliyaullah*) who reach that station, *maqam*, hide themselves. The story in the Holy Qur'an about al-Khidr ﷺ illustrates this truth. He did things people do not usually do; things that even the Prophet Moses ﷺ found difficult to accept. God instructs us by means of that example, to learn, not because Moses ﷺ is lower in station for after all, he is one of the five greatest Prophets. No one attains the level of the prophets and the Prophet's Companions (*Sahaba*). By informing us of Moses' ﷺ relation to Khidr ﷺ, the Qur'an wishes to give us the example of one brought near to God, one of His saints. Such individuals are just as the Holy Tradition describes them, *"My saints are under My domes; no one knows them except Me."* God Himself hides saints, since they are exceedingly precious to Him. Another Prophetic Tradition illustrates this:

---

[27] *Ibid.*, p. 4.

[28] *maqam*—what the servant realizes in his station in terms of spiritually-perfected manners, *adab*, and what is communicated... [al-Qushayri].

*Whoever comes against a Friend of Mine I declare war on him.*[29]

In the midst of people, God's Friends say and do things that others do not accept. That is the meaning of Ibn Ajiba's words, "No one bears such a person." For the same reason, when the Prophet Sayyidina Muhammad ﷺ came forth, his people rejected him. All prophets were rejected by their people. Since that is the case of the prophets what then can be expected for *awliya*? It is natural that they will be rejected completely by common people, because *awliya* are ordinary human beings upon whom God has bestowed heavenly power.

Today's religious scholars (*'ulama*) say there no longer remain any *awliya*. This is not true. Rather, these people have become blind so that they cannot see them. Why have they become blind? Because *awliya* have hidden themselves, especially in the present era. They know that no one will accept them and the power granted them by the Lord. If they display anything of what they have been empowered with, people come against them.

Thus the highest level of *wali*, is one who acts like normal people and does not appear different from them in aspect or behavior. Thus one of God's friends (*awliya*) behaves like others to the extent that people say about him, "He is like us. What is different?" What they don't know about him is that he has been tested by *awliya*; by the Prophet ﷺ, and finally by God the Exalted. He passed his tests and was given his spiritual trusts (*amanat*).

Ibn Ajiba ق continues: "nor does that person put up with [standards of behavior] others tolerate." This means he watches as they go astray, calling them to return to the Path, but they do not listen. After a while, the saint leaves them.

It is related that Bayazid al-Bistami ق, one of the greatest saints of Islam, was constantly worshipping God, ascending in closeness, until he could even hear the angels. He arrived at a station where he sought the Divine Presence saying, "O my Lord!

---

[29] Even the rigorous Ibn Taymiyya verified this Prophetic Tradition.

Open for me the gate to Your Divine Presence." He heard a voice in his heart saying, "O Bayazid! If you want to enter My Presence, you must become people's refuse pile."

Hence, al-Hasan ibn Mansour ق says here, "The elect servants of God are like the earth. They accept every type of refuse to be cast upon them and yet nothing issues from them but sweetness. Both the good and the sinner walk upon it."

The "earth" is characterized by strength. Whatever God Wills, the earth accepts. It has no will of its own. In this respect *awliyaullah* resemble the earth: "every vile and ugly thing is cast upon it," and it accepts. The Arabic word used, *qabih* does not mean just "vile" or "ugly" but rather, "rank" and "putrid" suggesting the worst refuse thrown on the earth. Yet, after he accepts it, the verse continues, "nothing comes from him except goodness."

The Friend of God (*wali*) does not treat you the same way you treat him. Rather he returns good for evil. It is related that Bayazid ق tested the doctors of law, with extreme ecstatic utterances, until at last they elected to stone him. This was due to their lack of understanding the station from which he was speaking. Bayazid ق was not someone inclined to commit heresy, for even Ibn Taymiyya praises his piety. But his intention was to test them, for they in fact had tried to test him.

Finally, when they had stoned Bayazid ق and left him for dead, his inert body was thrown in a garbage dump. Actually, he was still alive, but very weak. Eventually after lying injured in the dump seven days, he revived slightly and was able to move. He began searching about for something to eat. He found a bone, with a bit of fetid meat on it, probably thrown out one week before. When he took it a dog appeared growling and spoke to him, saying, "This is my territory, and this my food. You cannot touch it." Thus did God reveal to him the understanding of animal speech.

Bayazid ق relates, "I was beseeching God and saying, 'O God! O my Lord! What I have sought I sought only for the sake of Thy love. I willed for them to kill me but Thou quickened me and caused me to live. And once I regained my life I wished them to put me to death yet again; and that then Thou wouldst quicken me once more, and they would stone me yet another time. And again wouldst Thou revive me, over and over, because each time they stone me I would pray for them that Thou, My God, wouldst forgive them of their sins. So whatever Thou hast granted me of rewards for prayer and spiritual struggle, do Thou, O Lord, cause them to share in that same reward with me." This shows how much the Saint (*wali*) will love God's servants when he enters into His love.

Today many Muslim scholars say, "There are no more saints." In reality, they exist, but since only a few will understand their states, they are hidden. Another saying of today's scholars is, "Every person of faith (*mu'min*) is a saint (*wali*)." If that is the case, God would not differentiate between a person of faith and a saint.

In any case, who can truly say he is a believer (*mu'min*)? Do these scholars not recall God's saying in the Holy Qur'an:

> The Arabs say, "We believe." Say, "Ye have no Faith;
> but ye (only) say, 'We have submitted our wills to
> Allah,' For not yet has Faith entered your hearts. But if
> ye obey Allah and His Messenger, He will not belittle
> aught of your deeds: for God is Oft-Forgiving, Most
> Merciful."[30]

Who can grant one the certification that faith (*Iman*) has entered his heart? Such certification is not given from one Muslim to another; it is given from God to the believer.

Wherever they find themselves, God's saints build places of prayer, *zawiyas*, *khaniqas* or *ribats* (gathering places for spiritual training and practice). Once raised, people come from far and wide to visit them and they receive all in their meetings. They do not say, "We will not meet this one or that one." Today people

---

[30] Suratu 'l-Hujurat [The Private Apartments], 49:14.

30

say, "These individuals are enemies. We cannot meet them. These people cursed us, we cannot meet them." But the Prophet ﷺ came to all humankind—whether friendly or inimical to him.

*We have not sent thee but as a universal (Messenger) to men, giving them glad tidings, and warning them (against sin), but most men understand not.* [31]

If an enemy came to Prophet Muhammad ﷺ, he was obliged to open his door. As *awliyaullah* are inheritors of the Prophet's states and character, their doors must always be open. Else what is the benefit of sainthood (*wilayah*)? God bestowed Sainthood upon them in order to hear people out, to deal with them and to bring them to Islam. When you close your door and say, "I don't work with those people," you have isolated yourself and become a barrier to the Way. You have to work with people of any faith, any religion, and any group to convey them to Truth (*Haqq*). That is why Grand Shaykh 'Abd Allah al-Faiz ad-Daghestani ق met with everyone, and we seek to follow in his footsteps. You cannot close the door saying, "You are not a member." Now everything is based on paid membership—based on money. They tell you, "Pay fifty dollars and become a member." Nothing is done purely for God's sake any longer.

"Both good people and the ugliest of sinners walk over and step on the elect servant of God." That means he will carry burdens—he is everyone's garbage disposal. And in return, he offers prayers for people; in order to turn their hearts round to God. The elect servants of God try to do their best for people although people do their worst for them. That is why the good and the bad step on them and walk all over them.

Ibn Ajiba ق said, "And the vilest ones are they who pretend that they are an elect servant of God while failing in generosity." An elect servant of God does not fail in generosity. He is not stingy. A servant of God is always generous with the gifts his

---

[31] Surah Saba [Sheba], 34:28.

Lord has granted him or her, by not withholding it. God is the Most Generous of the generous (*Akram al-akramin*).

Similarly, the Prophet ﷺ is described by God as:

> *to the Believers is he most kind and merciful.*[32]

and

> *We sent thee not, but as a Mercy for all creatures.*[33]

This verse means that Prophet Muhammad ﷺ will ask God's forgiveness on everyone's behalf. In short, a servant of God cannot be stingy. The worst person is someone who pretends to be an elect servant of God and is stingy. Not stingy with his money, but stingy in carrying the difficulties of people and taking back for himself, whatever God gave him of rewards, as gifts to them.

Worse yet, are those of God's servants on whom he has bestowed the gifts of knowledge of the religion and its inner meanings and who withhold this knowledge from those who are capable of receiving it. These are the doctors of law that tell lies about God and pronounce permitted what He has prohibited. Of these, we have many examples today. They say, for example, that God wills people to lay down their lives in support of the corrupt or, serve false causes or to propagate wrong doctrine. These servants are the spiritually stingy. Such persons never succeed and on the Day of Judgment, they will be reckoned among the *losers*. They are like a tree covered with beautiful blossoms in spring, but which is infertile and fails to yield fruits in autumn.

To be perfectly clear, the true authorized servant of God carries the sins of those who are under his authority by asking God's forgiveness for those under him and by requesting God bestow whatever he received of rewards on them from whatever levels God has raised him to. That is for whoever comes to visit him.

---

[32] Suratu 't-Tawbah [Repentance], 9:128.
[33] Suratu 'l-Anbiya [The Prophets], 21:107.

The Prophet ﷺ said:

*God has angels roaming the roads seeking the people of His Remembrance (dhikr), and when they find a group of people reciting dhikr, they call each other and encompass them in layers until the first heaven...* **And someone not from them, but who came only for a certain issue, sits with them.** *God said, "no regrets will come to whoever sits with them."*[34]

That means that anyone coming for only a few minutes, even if he is not one of them, will be rewarded for being with them. Anyone who comes to the saint, the saint will give to him from what God and the Prophet ﷺ gave him. That is what it means—the opposite of stingy. It means giving what God adorned him with in the way of mercy. It means taking on and carrying the difficulties and problems of people who came to see him.

Now Ash-Shibli ق goes on to say, "The elect servant of God is disconnected from creation and connected to the Truth, *al-Haqq*." He continues, "his heart is cut off from people and connected with the Divine." At the most literal level, it means he severs himself from the creatures and connects himself spiritually with God's Love. But at a deeper level it also means that he rejects all that is false and loves all that is true. The servant of God does not involve himself in issues that do not concern him or in what people do and say contrary to the Truth. He is connected with Truth. He likes everything about Truth and dislikes whatever is false. When he disconnects himself from falsehood, he veils it, as if he is not seeing it, even while being perfectly aware of it. At the same time, he does not backbite and draw attention to the falsehood and wrongdoing perpetrated by people.

He connects himself to Truth and disconnects himself from falsehood. He does this in order to balance their falsehood by bringing Truth to the other side of the balance. Otherwise, if falsehood goes unchecked, it will cause disaster both in the

---

[34] *Sahih Bukhari* and *Sahih Muslim*.

Community and in the world. Thus the *awliya* are like mountains in the Community; they balance everything, as the mountains keep the earth in balance:

*And the mountains as pegs* [35]

If falsehood were to increase unchecked there would no longer be any balance in the world and it would turn upside down. Thus, the *awliya* bring everything into balance. For this reason God said:

*In order that ye may not transgress (due) balance. So establish weight with justice and fall not short in the balance.*[36]

These verses mean, "Make everything balanced in the scale." If the *awliya* do not balance falsehood by means of worship, if they do not balance what the workers of iniquity perpetrate in the way of falsehood with truth, this worldly material life, *dunya*, would have disappeared long ago.

Among the signs of Last Days, 'Abd Allah bin Amr Ibn al-'As related that the Prophet said:

*God will not take knowledge from the hearts of the scholars but he takes the scholars (they die). There will be no more scholars to take their place so people will take extremely ignorant leaders. They will be asked questions and will give fatwas (legal rulings) without knowledge. They are misguided and they misguide others.*[37]

The pious servants (*salihi*) have been balancing everything from the time of the Prophet . Indeed, throughout all ages, they are balancing falsehood with truth. But now that balance they have brought to the worlds is reaching its end so that there is no longer a balance. Indeed, the lack of a sense of proportion has become the dominant characteristic of our epoch. That is why today one sees so much killing. And while everyone speaks of

---

[35] Suratu 'n-Naba [The Great News], 78:7.
[36] Suratu 'r-Rahman [The Merciful], 55:8-9.
[37] *Sahih Bukhari* and *Sahih Muslim*.

peace, peace, peace, in fact everywhere people are dying. May God keep us under the wings of His pious servants whom He has endowed with knowledge and entrusted with the guidance of the community of Muhammad ﷺ and balance our deeds to be in a good way.

## BALANCING THE SELF

Balance begins with the self, for the self is the root of all spiritual troubles. In the approach to the Divine Presence, the seeker must build his or her divine aspect based on the spirit of the holy Prophetic Tradition:

> ...My servant draws not near to Me with anything more loved by Me than the religious duties I have enjoined upon him, and My servant continues to draw near to Me with supererogatory works so that I shall love him. When I love him I am his hearing with which he hears, his seeing with which he sees, his hand with which he strikes and his foot with which he walks...[38]

One may be fastidious in observing the obligations and in practicing supererogatory worship: making all the voluntary prayers and fasts, paying extra charity and practicing the Sunnah to excess. However, in the search for realities, even that is not enough. This is because often the worshipper will miss a critical step: that of self-examination, al-muhasabah.

Without this aspect, the very worship we do in the belief we are attaining higher levels can in fact become an obstacle to progress. How? When that worship is not absolutely pure, done for the sake of God Alone, and we continue to do it under the self-satisfied notion that we are doing all that is humanly possible to achieve spiritual progress. At that time, the self will have held sway for it relishes its "success" in spiritual work and discipline.

---

[38] Sahih Bukhari.

## THE HOUSE OF ILLNESS

Therefore, as with all illnesses there is a cure. In entering this discussion, we note the relevance of the Prophetic saying:

*The stomach is the house of all illnesses* and the source of all cures is diet.[iii]

Dieting means to be fully aware of what enters one's mouth and arrives at the stomach. The first step in dieting is to impose controls on the ego's desire to eat. This is found in implementing the Prophetic Tradition where the Prophet ﷺ said:

*We are a people who don't eat until we are hungry and when we eat we don't eat our fill.*[39]

True cleverness is possessed by the one who can prevent his hand from reaching out to eat more, such a person truly controls his ego. Egos always desire more—they are endlessly greedy. If God granted us a house, and the ego sees someone who owns a bigger house, it wants that house. The ego never says, "All praise be to God, we have a place to stay."

If someone has one million dollars the ego wants two million; if he has two million, it wants three million.

Yahya bin Yahya, a student of Imam Malik, asked him for advice. Imam Malik gave him three recommendations, each of which comprises a treasure. He said:

I will compose all the medicine of the physicians, and the entire fruit of the science of medicine in one sentence: withdraw your hand from eating as long as you have desire to eat.[40]

Following such advice one will never see sickness in his life. More importantly that is training the ego to listen to and accept the truth. For the battle with the ego begins with a conversation, a

---

[39] Related from 'Umar bin al-Khattab ؓ. Ibn Kathīr says its chain is weak, but the meaning is true.
[40] Arabic: *an tarfa yadak 'ani t-ta'am.*

debate between the soul, which yearns for spiritual attainment, and the ego, *nafs*, which always seeks satisfaction in the basest desires. The soul will ask the ego, "Are you done eating?" To which it replies, "No, I want another bite, for this food is so tasty." At that time the reproachful-self (*an-nafs al-lawwamah*) will say, "But you are not keeping the *Sunnah* of eating." That is the decision point: to observe the *Sunnah*, or not; to keep discipline or not; to control the ego or not.

It is for this reason that the Prophet ﷺ said:

*Contemplation for one hour is better than seventy years of worship.*[iv]

What you achieve by contemplation *tafakkur*, also known in Arabic as *muraqabah,* is to achieve what you cannot achieve even if you are performing voluntary worship for seventy years. It means that what is gained by meditation is unattainable through worship alone, for even Iblees, the condemned, busied himself with worship constantly such that not one handspan in heavens and earth remained without the traces of his prostration. Yet in the end he failed due to his rebellious ego, and spurred on by self-conceit he disobeyed a single order of His Lord and thus fell from grace.

Shaykh Abu 'l-Hasan ash-Shadili ق said, "The fruits of meditation (*muraqabah*) are the Divinely-gifted talents." But meditation cannot be done amongst the people, it must be done in isolation (*al-ʿuzlah*). That in fact, is the primary reason people sit in isolation: to do meditation.

Such meditation, completely secluded away from all other eyes and ears, will allow you train the ego, to ride it, as a horseman rides his mount. Then once you ride the ego, it can no longer control you. When you say, "I am not eating," it will say, "I hear and I obey." On the other hand, if you have not trained it, you will be overcome by your ego.

That is why a master may try his students by giving them excess food to eat. Such a trial is actually to combat the ego's desires to **not eat**, which comes about when the stomach is full and the food is not particularly delicious. In keeping the ways of Sufism nothing must accord with the ego's desires. So should the Shaykh order you to eat an entire pot of bland and tasteless food, you must do so willingly, for it is in obedience to the order that he will raise you.

However, if the Shaykh dispenses more food to you—food which is blessed by his hands, his prayers and his preparing it while invoking God and praising His Prophet ﷺ—and you indicate in even the slightest way, "That is enough," you are displaying your disobedience, struggling in fact to say, "No, I will not eat any more." Consider, if that is your reaction to something that cannot harm you what do you think if the Shaykh puts you to a more difficult trial?

This is all in regard to physical nourishment. If we observe dieting in regard to our physical constitution, what are we doing in regards to our spirit, which requires nourishment as well?

## DIETING FOR THE SOUL

Dieting for the soul means to prevent oneself from doing anything originating in bad desires; it will be a cure for one's spiritual dimension and a preparation for the afterlife.

People today do not diet for the soul. They are not examining the desires of the self and asking "How am I going to face God the Almighty and Exalted, on the Day of Examination, where He is going to ask us, 'Did you stop yourself from being greedy, from jealousy and from envy?'"

If someone is receiving his provision from God, then no one can prevent him from receiving his destined portion. If God has granted you one thousand of something then you will get your one thousand, even if one thousand others are seeking it; and if God has written for you ten, then it may be that someone else will get one thousand and you will get your destined ten. Never worry that someone else will eat your provision. With that in mind, jealousy and envy can never arise.

Thus it is said:

*Dieting is the head of all cures.*[41]

*Himyah* means dieting, but in this context it means preventing yourself from doing anything outside the bounds of the Sacred Law. Whatever you are doing that contravenes the Divine Law you must stop doing, else you will end up in a situation that you are happy in this life but in the afterlife you are full of regret.

The heart is an organ but its nourishment is not through eating. Rather the heart uploads and downloads. It gorges itself with the food of gossiping, dark whisperings, and evil promptings. If you give it bad spiritual food, it will be demolished, but if you give it healthful spiritual food, it will flourish. That is a choice each person must make.

Just as the stomach is the house of physical maladies, the heart is the house of spiritual malaises. So just as one diets as a cure for the physical body so to will observing the nourishment intake of the heart enable one to receive God's light.

It is related that God said:

*Neither My heaven nor My earth could contain Me, but the soft, humble heart of my believing servant can contain Me.*[v]

There cannot be two within the heart. God does not accept idolatry, though He may forgive anything less than that. What does He accept? Oneness. God does not accept that anyone associate with Him in His Divinity, for He is the Ultimate Sovereign King. God wants Absolute Oneness to be attributed to Himself. If there is even the slightest aspect of filth or impurity in the heart then no light will penetrate into your heart from God's lights. That would be unacceptable for God's lights can only be for Himself.

For this reason, the dieting of the heart consists of listening to a guided and guiding master, a *murshid*, who has the skill to

---

[41] Arabic: *al-himyatu ras ad-daw.*

disconnect the seeker from his own self-aggrandizing self and then, like a heart surgeon, carefully reconnect the seeker to his reality in the Divine Presence.

### BREAKING THE EGO'S PRIDE

As we said earlier, the seeker may make great strides of progress in attainment by means of voluntary worship. However, he or she will reach a limit that cannot be crossed, and that is the blockage of the self, for the self will use any means at its disposal to intercept the upward progress of the seeker. The cause of this is arrogance, for the self does not allow the soul to take precedence, claiming, on the pattern of Pharoah, *"I am your Lord most high!"*[42] For this the guide must use drastic means, like emergency surgery, to eliminate the tyrannical self. This is illustrated in another story about Bayazid ق:

> There was a man in Bistam who was always in Bayazid's assembly and he never separated from him. At the same time the man was a renowned scholar of the region. Once he said to Bayazid ق, "O master! For thirty years I have been fasting in the daytime and remained standing at night in prayers. I have left all my passions. But I feel in my heart nothing at all of what you are talking about, although I believe in what you say and I know that you are telling the truth."

> Bayazid ق replied, "Even if you fast for three hundred years and keep standing in night prayers for three hundred years while you are (in the state in which) I see you, you will not experience one atom of this knowledge." The man asked, "Why, O master?" Bayazid ق answered, "Because you are veiled by your own self."

> He asked, "Is there any medicine by which to remove this veil?" Bayazid ق told him, "Remove the clothes (of the

---

[42] Suratu 'n-Nazi'at [Those Who Pull Out], 79:24.

scholar) that you are wearing, put on this (ragged) cloak, attach a bag around your neck and fill it with chestnuts. Then gather children around you and say at the top of your voice, 'O children! Whoever will slap me once I will give one chestnut. And whoever slaps me twice I will give two chestnuts. And whoever will push me so I fall down I will give three chestnuts." Go the place where you are most respected and let everyone who knows you see you like this. Begin with this before all else, so that first you fall from prestige (jah) and cause your self to be humiliated."

That man (who was a scholar of renown) said, "Oh! Glory to God! Is it to someone of my stature you say such a thing?" Bayazid ق replied, "Stop, stop, stop! Now you are committing the irreparable sin of association with God, shirk!"

He continued, "Stop now, you see how loose your tongue is. Even with thirty years [of struggle in the Way] yet you cannot control it. When you control yourself by humiliating yourself and make it known that you are truly a Sufi, then you will be accepted."

Bayazid ق said, "After you do this I shall let you know what is suitable for you." The man said, "I am unable to do this!"

Bayazid ق had sought out the defect in his disciple's character, and exposed it to him, for when he said, "Oh! Glory to God!" it was as if he was putting himself besides God, as if to say, "I am above that as God is above His Creation."

This story illustrates the need to create a new way in your life, as mentioned to that scholar, by humbling and demeaning yourself.

*Therefore justify not yourselves: He knows best who it is
that guards against evil.*[43]

Do not ever uplift yourself or give excuses to yourself. For the
Best of Creation, Sayyidina Muhammad ﷺ, the Master of masters,
the Seal of Messengers, the perfect human being was humble. God
gave him ﷺ everything: He gave him ﷺ intercession; He made him
ﷺ the first in creation; He made him ﷺ the last to be sent; He made
his nation the best of nations; He forgave his nation their sins
large and small and vouchsafed for them Abode of Safety in the
afterlife; He made him ﷺ the first to be resurrected on Judgment
Day; He made him ﷺ the first to enter paradise, along with his
entire Community. All this and yet the Prophet ﷺ said:

*I am the Master of the sons of Adam on Judgment Day and I say
this without boasting.*[44]

For God's Messenger ﷺ had no pride, therefore despite being
the greatest of all, he was most pleased when His Lord called him
"My servant," *'abdi.*

Shaykh Muhammad Nazim Adil al-Haqqani

Lefke, Cyprus

Jumada al-Awwal 4, 1426 / June 10, 2005

---

[43] Suratu 'n-Najm [The Star], 53:32.
[44] Tirmidhi, Ibn Majah and Ahmad.

# INTRODUCTION
## THE JOURNEY TO DISCIPLESHIP

The Sufi masters have determined that four major factors influence every human being's character. These are lust, the ego, worldly desire and the whispers of Satan. This book addresses the latter three factors: ego, worldly desire and Satan's influence.

This book begins by describing the ruinous characteristics of the self, known as *nafs* in Sufi terminology. Everyone possesses some of these characteristics, while some possess all of them. How much they affect someone depends on the nature and personality of the individual, the environment around him, how he was affected by that environment and how he was polluted as he grew up. When someone begins to consider taking up the Path to the Divine Presence and following the way of Gnosticism, these characteristics become obstacles which must be eliminated. This process of wayfaring is known as seeking the Station of Perfected Character, *Ihsan*.

Initially, when the spirituality of the individual begins to call him and his soul begins yearning for its heavenly spiritual connection, it will begin to impact not only his psyche and emotional state, but also his body. At that time, the individual begins to realize there is a need to develop the spiritual dimension and he begins to search for a spiritual master to guide him. Ultimately, that yearning will overwhelm him and he will begin to search in earnest for such guidance. As soon as he begins that search, heavenly power from the Divine Presence will direct him to his spiritual guide, who is a master of the Path. Love will then begin to develop between the seeker and that guide, and in his heart he will grow connected to his master. As that relationship of love begins to grow, he begins to look at the personality of his teacher with great love. This love develops into a spiritual connection, so that he begins his spiritual journey in the state of unconditional love. Such love is not related to any desire, but is a purely Platonic, spiritual love between the teacher and the student. Thus, he enters what is known as the, the Circle of Unconditional Lovers, (da'irat al-muhibin). That is the circle of students at the first level of the Way: the Level of Love.

When that love begins to appear in him, the master is the center of the circle, and the students are each a point on its circumference. Each has his or her own connection to the center, the master. That means each has his own direction, or qiblah, that points towards his teacher. As that connection begins to become apparent to the seeker—as for the master, it has always been so— that radius becomes like a bridge or tunnel into which the seeker begins to step from the circumference of the circle. Upon making his first steps into that tunnel, he begins to discover countless bad characteristics within himself. These negative traits can be condensed into seventeen primary characteristics. He might possess some or all of the seventeen within himself. The student then begins to realize that his teacher does not possess these characteristics. As he discovers one characteristic after another, he begins to eliminate them. As he begins to eliminate them, he moves down the tunnel and becomes a "beginner in the circle of lovers on the spiritual journey."

Once he becomes a beginner, he needs to achieve ten steps to reach the level of disciple. Eliminating the seventeen characteristics takes the seeker from the level of lover to the level of beginner, mubtadi'. This book then elaborates ten steps which will take him to the first stage of discipleship, musta'id, and from there will take him to the level of full discipleship, murid.

When the seeker reaches the levels of a full disciple, he begins to receive ever more heavenly understanding, which will raise him through three Circles of Certainty. First it will take him to

Certainty of Knowledge, *'Ilmu 'l-Yaqin*; then to Certainty of Vision, *'Aynu 'l-Yaqin*; and finally he will reach the Reality of Certainty, *Haqqu 'l-Yaqin*. Thus, he ends up in the level of reality.

As soon as the seeker begins to ascend the ten stages, taking him from beginner to disciple, he begins to develop the Knowledge of Certainty and its effects begin to appear to him and in him. At that time, the veils begin to be removed. First he will receive the Power of Hearing; followed by the Power of Seeing and finally the Power of Experiencing Reality.

He moves from level of audio to the level of video, and then from analog to digital. This allows him to receive more knowledge in ever-increasing amounts. It will be as if he is living the past, present and future. He will be hearing, seeing and experiencing what others have gone through, as revealed to him by his master. It will not be like hearing someone tell him a story, rather, in these stages he will actually be living that story, as if he is part of it. He will not simply be viewing events, but will actually take part in them, beginning to feel and sense all that the actual participants did. This is a higher level. He will begin to feel with the people he meets just as if he is one of those present in that person's past. That is the first step to becoming, not just someone who is learning, but someone able to give knowledge and help others. It is also the first level of a spiritual healer. That is why the healer can feel and sense with the patient, and for that reason he is able to powerfully support those who are ill, whether spiritually or physically.

As he inherits spiritual abilities from his mentor, someone who has previously mastered the Way, the disciple will begin to have the power to sense and experience the lives of others. If they are experiencing difficulties, suffering depression or feeling spiritually uplifted, he will feel it. He becomes part of them, so he knows what they need. This will allow him to build others. As well, it will lift him up to reach the level of the six realities of the heart described in the final section of the book, at which time the seeker has advanced from beginner, *mubtadi'*, to initiate, *musta'id*, and has arrived at the level of disciple, *murid*.

## THREE LEVELS OF FOLLOWING

The following story while often repeated will bear retelling here to illustrate these three stages of followership on the Sufi Path of Self-realization, and the level of certainty that accompanies each level.

Once a Daghestani wrestler came to our Grandshaykh 'Abd Allah ق and said, "O my shaykh, I want to take the Sufi path from you." That person came to the shaykh wearing huge daggers and swords. Daghestanis are extremely tough people, and they wear their moustaches big, pointing upwards, as a symbol of ego. That man came with all his ego, requesting the shaykh to make him a Naqshbandi disciple, *murid*. Grandshaykh said at first, "I shall never give you initiation in this way!" The man answered, "What! I am wearing a sword and several daggers, and I can defeat anyone! I want the path! If you don't give it to me, I shall beat you!"

Grandshaykh used his spiritual vision, *firasah*, to observe his heart, and immediately understood that the wrestler had good intentions. The order came that, despite being an armed wrestler, he was to be accepted as a student in the Path. Grandshaykh said, "I cannot give you the Path unless you faithfully fulfill my orders. However, before even that, I am sending you downtown for training."

Grandshaykh ordered that wrestler to go to the meat market and find a laborer whose job was to carry lamb intestines. "Go behind him and slap him on the neck with the flat of your hand. See what he says and report to me." The wrestler was very happy with the task before him, thinking, "If this is the Sufi Path, praise God, I will slap and punch my way to my spiritual secrets!" He said, "Of course, O my shaykh! This is my job. I will gladly go and slap him, not once, but hundreds of times!" "No," said Grandshaykh, "only once!"

The wrestler went downtown looking for the laborer. He found him, came up to him from the back, raised his hand, and slapped him on the neck with all his strength. That person turned, looked at him, but said nothing, and continued on his way. The wrestler could see anger in his eyes; however, he had expected a stronger reaction: in which case he would have felt justified to hit him two, three or four times, or knock him out with a good punch. Instead all he could do was return to the shaykh and report, "My shaykh, I saw something very extraordinary today. When I beat that man, he did not react, but only looked at me with anger. I waited for him to come at me in order to finish him off, but he never did!"

The next day, Grandshaykh told him, "Go now to the same place downtown. You will find another worker selling lamb stomachs." He continued, "With this one, you may use more force and roughness when you beat him. See what he says and come back and tell me." "O my shaykh," the wrestler answered, "your order is my desire! I will beat everyone for you! This is a very easy order."

He went downtown, found the person the shaykh told him about, and with all his power, knocked him down with a strong blow. The man fell down along with all the meat he was carrying. While still on the ground, he turned around and smiled at the wrestler, but said not a word. Then he picked up the meat and left. The wrestler was angrier now than with the first man. "Why," he thought to himself, "did that person not react? Then I would have taken my dagger and finished him off." He came back to his shaykh and told him of this event.

The next day, Grandshaykh said, "I am sending you to a farm where you will find a very old man plowing the field. Now don't use your hand, because this is an old man. He needs something better: you have to use a stick on him!" The shaykh continued,

"Use all your power, and let your stick break on his back! Don't come back to me if you don't break the stick on his back."

Now the heart of that wrestler began to change. But he did not reject the order of the shaykh. He took the stick and went, but he now he felt afraid. "Why must I beat that old person?" he thought to himself. Nevertheless he went to the field and found him, as the shaykh had said, plowing the field. He came up behind him, and remembered the shaykh's orders to break the stick on the old man's back. He was overcome by mixed feelings, of happiness and sadness at the same time; though in the first two incidents he had been thoroughly happy.

He took the stick and brought it down on the old man's back. But because of his disquiet, he did not hit him with sufficient strength to break the stick. As soon as he struck the farmer, the farmer struck the plow with his foot in order to plow more quickly, without even looking behind him. The wrestler thought, "I must break the stick!" With all his power now, he struck the farmer again, but still the stick did not break. The farmer, in his turn, struck down the plow with all his power and the cow moved faster, until the farmer was dragged to his knees. But the wrestler had orders to break the stick, so he raised the stick for the third time and, with all the power he could summon, slammed it on top of the old man's back and broke the stick.

The poor old man fell down; then immediately got to his knees and came crawling to the wrestler. He seized his hand with the words, "Please, give me your hand and let me kiss it. Because of my sins, my shaykh has sent you to me in order to correct me. I know I am making mistakes and you were an instrument for my correction." The old man said this although he was in not need to be corrected, because he was already a "corrected" person: he had attained the stage of discipleship, *murid*, in the Naqshbandi Sufi Way, which means that he had attained a high degree. He continued, "I caused your hand to feel pain by having to beat me harder. Please forgive me, and do not speak against me in the Judgment Day, in the presence of God, in the presence of the

Prophet ﷺ and in the presence of my shaykh! I am ashamed before my shaykh, who sent you to me to correct me. Please forgive me for causing pain to your hand." He did not even mention his own back.

It was as if he had thrown cold water on that wrestler. He was melting. He went back to Grandshaykh feeling greatly ashamed. Once there, Grandshaykh told him to sit and explained, "O my son, the first man you met was a beginner in the Path, *mubtadi'*. When you slapped him, he only looked at you, but he looked with anger. It means he knows that I am sending you to correct him, but he still has anger in his heart, and that is why you can see it on his face. The second one is at the level of one 'ready' to enter and become one 'prepared' in the Way, *musta'id*. When you hit him, he looked at you, but he was laughing, and this shows that there yet remains his will, as if he were saying, 'O my shaykh, I know that this is from you and I am laughing. You are testing me, and I am going to resist.' Therefore there is still a will there."

"That old person of eighty years," Grandshaykh went on to say, "is a disciple—*murid*—in our Order, because he sees everything as coming from his shaykh; not from X, Y or Z."

Then Grandshaykh 'Abd Allah ad-Daghestani ق said to the wrestler, "O my son, this is not enough; I am going to take you for a picnic. Come with me." Now comes the most important wisdom. That wrestler who had come by way of punching and beating everyone, at the end of the three days, had become an ant whom everyone could trample underfoot and crush. From what Grandshaykh had shown him, his pride and ego had dropped.

Grandshaykh took him to an orchard full of apple-trees. "O my son," he said, "Look at that tree full of apples. Now take that big stone and throw it against the tree and see how it will react."

The wrestler understood this example. Throwing the stone represented his physical power, and his urge to assault everyone.

The wrestler took the stone and hurled it against the apple-tree. The blow was so powerful that one of the apple-tree's branches broke and fell, along with ten apples. The shaykh said,

"My son, what have you done? You have harmed that tree by throwing that stone at it and breaking that branch. You hurt, broke, injured, punched and killed! But what did that tree do to you? It sent you ten apples in return, each one sweeter than the other."

The wrestler understood wisdom behind this example. The tree's utter acceptance of the breaking of its branches and dispensing its fruits for all to eat from, represented those who leave their will for their teacher's.

This means that if anyone harms you, you should return his harm with good. If someone hurt you, you must say, "O my Lord, O my Prophet ﷺ, O my master! That person hurt and harmed me; because he harmed me, you are going to give me rewards. That reward, I am giving back to him, and I am sacrificing that reward to him in order that he will be better. I am giving everything to him." This is what the Prophet ﷺ said we must do when he said:

*None of you is a believer until he loves for his brother what he loves for himself,*[45]

and the teachings of the Naqshbandi order "love for your brother more than what you love for yourself." When someone hurts you, you have to repay it with a reward.

Within this story is a final lesson. The fruits of the tree give the ultimate sacrifice, for they are consumed and thus leave existence. However in doing so, Mawlana Shaykh Nazim ق revealed the inner secret: they leave behind seeds, which falling on fertile earth will sprout forth and eventually produce not another apple, but a garden of apple trees, giving countless apples year after year.

Explaining this process, Mawlana Shaykh Nazim ق said:

It is only one seed you plant, yet after a while you look and see that instead of the seed, there is something below ground and something above ground coming up, but the seed has disappeared. It is demonstrating that secret

---

[45] Bukhari and Muslim.

wisdom that was placed in it by its Creator: that when it sacrificed itself to be nothing, then its Creator granted to that seed roots, and above the ground branches and leaves, which growing up and growing up, until after a while, fruits are coming. Then, when you look at the fruits, you find dozens of seeds in each one. How can it be? Because that seed sacrificed itself to be nothing. When it accepts to be nothing, God grants to that seed to multiply; all arranged in such a perfect fashion as mentioned in the Qur'an:

> *See you not how God sets forth a parable? - A goodly word like a goodly tree, whose root is firmly fixed, and its branches (reach) to the heavens,- of its Lord. It brings forth its fruit at all times, by the leave of its Lord. So Allah sets forth parables for men, in order that they may receive admonition.*[46]

And:

> *The parable of those who spend their substance in the way of Allah is that of a grain of corn: it groweth seven ears, and each ear Hath a hundred grains. Allah giveth manifold increase to whom He pleaseth: And Allah careth for all and He knoweth all things.* [47]

Such are the Guiding Shaykhs of the Way, for they take on the burdens of their followers, spending of their own selves— meaning from the spiritual treasures God has granted them—and using all they possess, transform their followers like seeds, they bring forth new generations which provide abundance and blessings anew.

---

[46] Surat Ibrahim [Abraham], 14:24, 25.
[47] Suratu 'l-Baqara [The Cow], 2:261.

# الاخلاق الذميمة

## THE SEVENTEEN RUINOUS TRAITS
### AL-AKHLAQU 'DH-DHAMIMAH

# THE TREE OF BAD MANNERS

When Imam Muhammad al-Busayri ق asked Shaykh Abu'l-Hasan al-Kharqani ق about the number of major ruinous traits in human character, the latter replied they number seventeen. Each of these traits resembles a great tree, for each has a trunk, which is deeply rooted; and each has primary branches, smaller off-shooting branches, leaves and so on. Each tree is laden with various kinds of bad manners. Here we will examine these seventeen negative characteristics, which the Sufi master Abu 'l-Hasan al-Kharqani ق categorized by the measure of their impact on the overall human character.

The following Prophetic narration (*hadith*) describes seven of these negative traits and the resulting drastic consequences which befall God's servants, who, though observing acts of piety and devotion, are in fact only harming themselves.

Al-Faqih said, "I asked Muʿadh ibn Jabal ◉, 'Tell me a hadith which you had heard from the Prophet, and which you have memorized and remembered every day since you heard it.' He started crying until I thought he would never stop, and then he said:

> I said to the Prophet ﷺ one day while I was sitting close to him, "May my mother and father be a sacrifice for you, O Messenger of God. Tell me something!" He raised his head to the heavens and said, "Praise be to God who decrees for His creation as He likes."
>
> Then he ﷺ said, "O Muʿadh!" I said, "At your service! O Messenger of mercy and the leader of goodness."
>
> He ﷺ said:

*I will relate to you a hadith which no other prophet has told his nation; if you remember it, it will benefit you; but if you hear it and forget it, you would have no excuses with God on Judgment Day.*

He ﷺ continued:

*Before God created the seven heavens and the earth, He created seven angels. For each heaven there is an angel standing before its gate. The Guardian Angels write the deeds of a certain servant from morning until night. They then raise his deeds, blazing like the sun, to the lowest heaven purifying them and adding to them. There the angel (at its gate) will say, "Stop! Go and throw these deeds back in the face of their owner, and tell him, 'May God never forgive you.' I am in charge of backbiting, and he is someone who backbites the believers. I will not let his deeds ascend past me to the farther heavens."*

Then he ﷺ said:

*The Guardian Angels will raise the shining deeds of another servant to the second heaven. The angel (at its gate) will say, "Stop! Throw these deeds back in the face of their owner, and tell him, 'May God never forgive you!' because he sought with his deeds the material world. I am in charge of the deeds of the lower world, dunya, and I will not let his deeds ascend beyond me."*

Then he ﷺ said:

*The Guardian Angels will raise the deeds of a servant—deeds with which he was pleased such as charity and much prayer—up to the third heaven. The angel at its gate will say, "Stop! Throw these deeds back in the face of their owner, and tell him, 'May God never forgive you!' I am in charge of arrogance, and he is someone who was arrogant when he was with people. God has ordered me never to let his deeds go past me."*

He ﷺ continued:

*The Guardian Angels would raise the deeds of a servant, deeds of excessive prayers and fasting—shining like the stars—up to the fourth heaven where its angel will say, "Stop! Throw these deeds back in the face of their owner, and tell him, 'May God never forgive you!' I am the angel responsible for pride in one's deeds.*

*God ordered me to never allow the deeds in which there is self-gratification go past me." The angels will throw those deeds back in the servant's face and will continue to curse him for three days.*

*He ﷺ said:*

*The Guardian Angels, along with other angels, will raise up the deeds of a servant, his struggle in God's Way and his voluntary prayers observed between the obligatory ones—moving like a bride on the way to meet her groom—until they reach the fifth heaven. There the angel of the fifth heaven will order them, "Stop! Go and throw the deeds of that servant back in his face, and load them upon his back. Tell him, 'May God never forgive you.' He envied those who were studying and working for the sake of God, and wronged them." His Guardian Angels will place them upon that servant's back and will curse him as long as he remains alive.*

*He ﷺ then said:*

*The Guardian Angels will raise the deeds of a servant, who served God devotedly—maintaining an unbroken state of ritual purity, observing the night vigil and performing excessive worship—until they reach the sixth heaven, where its angel will tell them, "Stop! Go and throw the deeds of their owner back in his face. I am the angel in charge of mercy. Your friend here did not have mercy towards anything. If difficulty or tragedy befell one of God's servants, he was happy. My Lord has ordered me never to let his deeds go beyond me."*

*He ﷺ then said:*

*The Guardian Angels will raise up the deeds of a servant—his veracity, striving and piety—up to the seventh heaven, their light blazing forth like lightning. They would reach the seventh heaven, where its angel will tell them, "Stop! Go and throw the deeds of this servant back in his face, and lock up his heart. I am the angel of veiling; I veil away every deed which is not done for God's sake. He sought high status from his deeds, to be remembered in gatherings and with a good name in the cities. God has ordered me never to let his deeds ascend past me."*

*He ﷺ then said:*

*The Guardian Angels will ascend with the deeds of a servant, who observed excellent conduct, held his tongue and made much remembrance of God. The angels of the heavens will fill its space until they reach below the Throne, all bearing witness on behalf of that servant. There God will say to them, "You are the angels observing My servant's deeds, but I am the Observer over what is within his soul. He did not seek My Face[48] with his deeds, he sought another's. My curse is upon him." The angels will respond, "Your curse and ours is upon him." Then the inhabitants of the heavens will say, "Upon him is God's curse, the curse of the seven heavens and earths, and our curse."*

*Muʿadh ibn Jabal [relating the hadith], began to cry. I asked, "O Messenger of God what should I do?"*

*He ﷺ said:*

*Follow the example of your prophet, O Muʿadh. Reach to certainty even if there are shortcomings in your deeds, and withhold your tongue from backbiting your brothers. Let your sins be yours, do not make your brother carry them. Do not praise yourself by speaking badly of your brothers. Do not raise yourself by putting down your brothers, and do not do your deeds for anyone to see."[49]*

This hadith demonstrates how so many of God's servants—while performing excessive and constant worship in all its many forms—may fall into self-destruction unawares, due to the spiritual maladies which permeate the very core of their selves. For this reason, shaykhs of the Naqshbandi Way insist on treating these illnesses in their followers, one-by-one, until they are eliminated. Anything short of this will result in the servant falling short of the goal of achieving God's Divine pleasure.

---

[48] i.e. perform them purely for God.

[49] Al-Faqih said: I heard a number of scholars who related this narration back to Khalid bin Midan.

## 1. ANGER (AL-GHADAB)

*A man said to Prophet Muhammad ﷺ, "Advise me." He replied,*
*"Do not become angry."*[50]

Anger is the worst of all seventeen of the ruinous traits. It may easily be said that anger is the source from which the others flow. That is why, in the story of Grandshaykh and the wrestler, the levels of followership were indicated by the different student's reaction to testing with anger.

When a person is overpowered by anger it is akin to intoxication. His anger takes him far from his normal pattern of thinking, and he becomes unable to reason rationally. Even in those states belonging to the other sixteen negative characteristics, one may still think rationally, plan what to do next and evaluate consequences. But when one is lost in the state of anger, one loses the ability to listen to reason, follow good judgment or accept advice. That is why the Prophet Muhammad ﷺ said to his dear companion Abu Bakr as-Siddiq ﷺ:

*Anger is a form of unbelief.*

And God said:

*Those who control their wrath and are forgiving toward*
*mankind; God loveth the good.*[51]

---

[50] Bukhari.
[51] Surat Ali 'Imran [The Family of 'Imran], 3:134.

Referring to its opposite, God here mentions those who are able to control their anger. Moreover, God makes it clear that those who forgive the ones who incite their anger, will be rewarded by Him.

The saints teach that anyone who wants to eliminate anger from their character must count how many times his or her temper is lost each day, even mildly. This is precisely why the Prophet ﷺ confirmed:

> *If you contemplate in isolation for one hour, God will reward you as if you worshipped Him with voluntary devotion for seventy years.*[52]

Any person engaged in such a struggle, with such intention and commitment, will receive this reward. Such seekers must reflect on how many times they became angry during the day and resolve to do better tomorrow: "I got angry because of this, so tomorrow I will try my best not to make the same mistake, so at least I will eliminate one fault." Anyone seeking to eliminate anger from their character must continue in this way, examining how many times they became angry and what caused it, thereby eliminating one fault after another. Then God will support that person, and the saints will be praying for them.

## A VISIT TO THE SULTAN OF THE SAINTS

With anger, a person forgets about God, about the Prophet ﷺ, about loved ones—even about one's shaykh and his guidance.

When I was young, my brother and I traveled to Damascus to visit our Grandshaykh, 'Abd Allah al-Fa'iz ad-Daghestani ق, may God sanctify his soul. We stayed with Grandshaykh for several hours before returning to our home in Lebanon, which took several hours more. At that time, I was a university student, and as we had not taken permission from our mother to visit

---

[52] *Nuzhat al-Majalis*. Similar Prophetic Traditions with variant wording are narrated in ad-Daylami and Abu ash-Shaykh.

Grandshaykh, she was upset when we returned. We became upset in turn, and when she started shouting, we shouted as well. We left the house in anger, like so many children do today when angry with their parents—though typically for reasons other than such religious issues.

Having quarreled with our mother, my brother and I returned to Damascus. To reach Grandshaykh 'Abd Allah's house, you must climb roads so steep that stairs run alongside them for pedestrians. We climbed at least 120 steps to reach his holy place on the mountain, Jabal Qasiyun.

Concerning this mountain, it is said that the Companions of the Cave[53] are buried there. The cave where Cain killed Abel—is also said to be there, and they say drops of water still drip from the ceiling of that cave, as if the cave itself were crying from the horror and sorrow of that event. Thus it can be said that this mountain is a living testimony to the worst fruits of anger.[vi]

High on this mountain, overlooking Damascus, is the Station of the Forty, the place of Budala ash-Sham, the forty saints in charge of managing the world's affairs, who come in spirit every night to pray at their respective niches.[vii] In addition, the Prophet Dhul-Kifl ﷺ is buried there, as well as the great saint Ibn al-'Arabi ق. Thus, of all the sacred places in the world, it is indeed one of the holiest.

So, we went up this mountain to the station of our Grandshaykh and up another set of stairs, through his meeting place where guidance is given, through his private house set apart from his meeting place, and then further inside to his room. We arrived at his personal quarters, yet before we could knock on his door, Grandshaykh 'Abd Allah ق opened it, looked at us and said, "I don't like anyone to visit me with anger! Go back to your mother! Ask for forgiveness. If she forgives both of you, then you may come. There is no other way to enter my home!" The door closed.

---

[53] C.f. Suratu 'l-Kahf [The Cave], 18: 9-26.

The saints cannot tolerate anger because it interferes with the connection between disciple and shaykh, student and teacher, devotee and master; it will close that door, and not only that door. Because the shaykh is your door to the Prophet ﷺ, anger closes the door between you and the Prophet ﷺ, and by closing your door to the Prophet ﷺ, your door to God is closed. That is why the Prophet ﷺ said:

*"The killer and the killed are both in Hellfire." The Companions said, "O Messenger of God! It is alright for the killer, but what about the one who was killed?" He said, "The killed one was [also] eager to kill his opponent."*[54]

Since both had the same intention, to kill the other, both deserve punishment, one more than the other.

On the other hand, from the spiritual interpretation of this Prophetic Tradition, the killed here then, is the one who killed his spiritual self, by oppressing it with anger. Thus his soul is killed by the ego's anger and the killer, his ego, is also left in the hell of its fiery nature.

Anger makes you heedless and reckless. In a state of anger, you will not listen to your father or your mother, to your brother or your sister, to your friend or your neighbor or to anyone. It will take away the light that is between you and the shaykh.

My brother and I returned to Lebanon, and we asked our mother's forgiveness. She forgave us and prayed for us. After two or three days, we sought her permission to go visit Grandshaykh 'Abd Allah ق and she gave it. We came to Grandshaykh, who greeted us and said, "Ah, now I will let you enter, and I will tell you something very important that normally I never reveal, but by order of the Prophet ﷺ, I am saying it to you."

Mawlana Shaykh Nazim ق was also present, and Grandshaykh 'Abd Allah ق proceeded to explain to us what the Prophet ﷺ has given someone at the level of Guide of Training,

---

[54] Bukhari.

*Murshid at-Tarbiyya*, the shaykh who is authorized to train disciples and advance their spiritual levels. He gives them permission to observe his disciples all the time—as the disciple must be under the supervision of the shaykh every moment of each day and night, twenty-four hours a day, seven days a week, without a single moment's neglect. Even if the shaykh has one million disciples, he will observe all of them simultaneously. He can always reach them, even if they number a hundred million.

How is it possible? Because this power is from the Prophet ﷺ, to whom God gave the power to observe all his Community (*ummah*)—dead or alive—in every moment. Grandshaykh explained to us that the Prophet ﷺ watched over the entire Community while he was here in the physical world, and even now from the other life the Prophet ﷺ can see us at every instant. For this reason, God gave him the title Witness, Shahid.[55] About this power of Witnessing, God said:

*We have sent to you (O men!) a messenger, to be a witness against you...*[56]

And the Prophet's perception is put on par with that of the Lord of the worlds, Who sees and encompasses all on the one hand and, on the other, that of all the living believers when He says:

*Allah and His Messenger will see your conduct.*[57]

And:

*Act! Allah will behold your actions, and (so will) His Messenger and the believers.*[58]

And the Prophet ﷺ said:

---

[55] Suratu 'l-Muzzammil [The Enshrouded One], 73:15.
[56] Suratu 'l-Muzzammil, 73:15.
[57] Suratu 't-Tawbah [Repentance], 9:94.
[58] Suratu 't-Tawbah, 9:105.

*My life is a great good for you: you will relate about me and it will be related to you. And my death is a great good for you: your actions will be exhibited to me, and if I see goodness I will praise God, and if I see evil I will ask forgiveness of Him for you.*[59]

From the power that God gives him, the Prophet ﷺ gives power to the shaykh to observe his followers in this manner; and the shaykh looks. That is one of the meanings in the Prophetic Tradition:

*Fear the vision of the believer, for verily he sees with the Light of God.*[60]

Grandshaykh ʿAbd Allah ق said:

This is our authority, given to us by the Prophet. Naqshbandi Guiding Shaykhs (*murshidin*) have permission to check their disciples three times in each twenty-four hour period, to give them a sense that they are being tested. The shaykh creates a situation where the disciple finds himself in difficulty; as their anger overtakes them, they are observed in their reactions. He observes if a disciple is patient and realizes, "Oh! I'm being tested. My shaykh is looking at me, my Prophet ﷺ is looking at me, my Creator is looking at me," and then lets go of anger for God's sake; or overreacts and forgets about his shaykh, his Prophet ﷺ and his Creator, and follows the anger of his ego, saying, "I am my own master and will do as I please!" In only an instant he will fail that test, and the shaykh must record that result. Then the shaykh will present another opportunity, a second test within that twenty-four hours, then a third, to see how rude the disciple is, if he uses harsh language and if he speaks as if he is authorized

---

[59] Al-Qadi ʿIyad  cites it in *al-Shifa,* Al-Bazzar in his *Musnad,* and as-Suyuti declared it sound.
[60] Tirmidhi (*hasan*).

to correct all others. While the shaykh is testing a disciple, he may also use the actions of that disciple to test another.

You must burn down this, the greatest tree from among all the ruinous traits within your heart, by keeping anger down, like a dog. If you restrain a dog in a very small room with every opening closed, leaving him only food and water, he will bark and bark. After one or two days, however, he will stop barking. That urge will die. If you let your anger bark, bark, and bark, allowing it to rage in your heart, and appear in your features, or worse be expressed on your tongue, you will be ruined by its overwhelming strength. Anger will control your thoughts and perceptions. Yet, if you begin to control your anger by keeping quiet, not allowing it to reach your tongue and not giving it control of your actions, anger will dissipate. At that time, the spiritual form of your shaykh will appear in front of you, and when this happens, the spirituality of the Prophet ﷺ takes control by completely calming down that anger. For that reason, the Prophet ﷺ said:

*If any of you becomes angry, let him keep silent.*[61]

Anger extinguishes the light of faith, leaving no more spirituality in your heart. Under anger's influence, everything you do will be dry, only a form that does not benefit you. God will still grant you Paradise for fulfilling your religious obligations, but you will never reach the higher level, spiritual ecstasy.

Anger is the dangerous secret of every spiritual disease, like the cancer that spreads to every cell of the body. Someone may have a tumor; when it is first discovered it is small, but if it is not removed it is likely to grow. Anger is like a small tumor, hidden in the heart of human beings through which Satan enters. The Archangel Gabriel came to the Prophet ﷺ when he was young, opened his heart, and removed that speck related to Satan. Thus, all human beings have that speck, except the Prophet Muhammad

---

[61] Bukhari, *Musnad* Ahmad.

🐝, for his personal devil accepted faith, and turned from evil.[viii] If you do not remove that speck of anger inside you, it will grow to extinguish the light of faith in your heart, and thus Satan will take a share from all your actions.

May God protect us from anger.

حب الدنيا

## 2. LOVE OF THIS WORLD
## (*HUBBU 'D-DUNYA*)

Jesus Christ ﷺ said:

*The love of this world is the root of every sin.*[62]

When someone in a high spiritual state reaches ecstasy, the sustenance he receives is spiritual, completely filling body and soul. At such a stage, this world and all its pleasures have no more value than spittle. Such a person lives each moment receiving continuous ecstasy and pleasure from God's Attribute of Beauty (*siffatu 'l-jamal*). To such a person, everything is for God, and the entire world is nothing compared to His Beauty, even though the entire world is created from this Attribute and proceeds from the Ocean of His Beauty. Yet this person drowns in the Source of that Beauty, so this world becomes meaningless to him. He is in a state of ultimate bliss and happiness.

In contrast, those who are in love with this world find it is the cause of troubles and disasters. A poet once wrote, "This world is a carcass, a rotten piece of flesh thrown in the street. Those who pursue it are scavenging dogs." Those who love this world and spend their time seeking more of it, are like scavengers running to devour a carcass. This is the view of a sincere person, who is in full ecstasy with his Lord and happy with his simple life. For such a person, to glorify and worship God sincerely, to give charity and

---

[62] Imam Ahmad.

to build a life in the hereafter is preferable. He prefers to be with people remembering God, than to be acquiring a portion, however small, of this world's glittering life, for as the Prophet ﷺ said:

*If people gather together in a circle mentioning God, God mentions them in a circle better than theirs.*[63]

Today, people apply perfumes to smell nice, unaware that angels are running from the stench of their bad deeds. They do not know that the saints run from the foul smell given off by the love of this world. If you do more for this world than you do for the world to come, this confirms your love for this world. In spirituality, holding on to anything that is more than you can eat today—even the sustenance that you keep for tomorrow—is considered evidence of your love for this world. Therefore it is better to offer it in the Way of God. If you possess more than today's sustenance, such excess is permissible if you give some of it in God's Way.

The Naqshbandi Sufi master Shah Naqshband ق was very rich. God gave him wealth because he did not waste it; he knew the value of wealth and he preserved it. His example was one of discipline. God gives wealth to the saints because they do not waste it for nonsense. Do not ask why you do not have what another one has; it may be that God is giving more to that person because he is more pious or more respectful of His gifts. Perhaps if God gives you such wealth, you will become the worst person on Earth.

To protect yourself from the love of this world, do not look at what others have; it is not your concern. Look at yourself and what you have. You are going to answer to God for that, not for others.

## THE LOYALTY OF DOGS

Let us look at the example of Shaykh Abdul Wahhab Sha'rani ق, who would check his house for leftover food every night before he slept. If he found any, he distributed it to the needy, without

---

[63] Muslim.

leaving himself anything for the next day. Once a person came to his home while he was in the mosque and gave the shaykh's daughter some meat, which she placed on top of a kitchen cabinet. When Shaykh Abdul Wahhab Sha'rani ق returned home that night, he looked to find what he could distribute to the poor. He gave what he found, only then retiring to his room to sleep. Oddly, that night he was unable to rest; he sensed there was something in his house that he had neglected to distribute. Finally, he got up and searched the house, up and down. He found the meat, his daughter had placed on the cabinet. He took it from the house, but found the street empty and everyone asleep. Search as he may, he could locate no one in need. He did, however, notice that dogs were running about, here and there. Finally he cut the meat into pieces and fed the dogs with it.

There is a Prophetic Tradition of the Prophet ﷺ, concerning a thirsty dog and a man drinking from a nearby well. Upon seeing the dog's state, the man lowered his shoe into the well and filled it with water for the dog. God forgave that man because he gave water to a thirsty dog.[64]

After Shaykh Abdul Wahhab Sha'rani ق fed all the dogs, they followed the shaykh home contentedly wagging their tails. He left them outside while he slept. In the early morning hours, he proceeded to the mosque to lead his followers in the morning prayer. His followers were astounded to see dozens of dogs following him to the mosque, and they started to chase the dogs away. Shaykh Abdul Wahhab Sha'rani ق scolded them, saying, "Why are you chasing them away? Do you think you are better than they? I gave them food only once and they became loyal to me. I give all of you spiritual sustenance every day and you are still not loyal to me."

---

[64] Bukhari.

الحقد

## 3. MALICE (AL-HIQD)

The Messenger of God ﷺ said:

*Do not have malice for one another.* [65]

And the cure for this negative trait, he related in another Tradition:

*Whoever looks at his brother with love, no malice will exist in his heart.* [66]

A community following the Way of God—the way of the Prophet Muhammad ﷺ, the Companions and the saints—never develops destructive intentions, because in such an ideal community, everyone seeks the Straight Path. However, when someone yields to their bad characteristics and lusts after what someone else has, they develop hatred and the intention of harming. Thus malice is something that is cultivated, as opposed to mere feelings of dislike that arise involuntarily at times.

In the Chapter of the Cave, we read the example of two men.[67] God gave one of them a garden filled with dates. He was very proud, and said to the other, "I am wealthier than you, in both money and children. I made this garden and I own it." Although it was a gift from God, his garden became to him like the houses

---

[65] Ibn Majah and *Musnad* Ahmad.
[66] Related by Ibn 'Abbas.
[67] Suratu 'l-Kahf [The Cave], 18:3 2-44.

and cars of people today, a source of pride. He entered his garden arrogant, like Pharaoh.

God is always against the tyrant. Although he may give tyrants time to bask in their arrogance and oppress others, He will never leave them unpunished, either in this world or the next. The love of this world leads to hatred, and this hatred may even develop into hatred against God and denial of the Judgment Day. Like the man to whom God gave that beautiful garden, such people think, "There is no God. I am the one who made this paradise. No one has better than what I have."

As it is narrated in the Qur'an, God inspired that man's neighbor. He was sincere and did not have such love for this world. He was not angry, so he did not develop hatred. The neighbor answered, "Why do you say such things? Do you not remember that God created you from earth? You are coming against your Lord! God is greater than you, and greater than everyone. If you enter your garden saying, 'This is from the Will of God,' it is better. Remember that garden is from God. God may destroy what He gave you, and give me something better."

Ultimately, God brought all that tyrant's garden to ruin and gave his believing neighbor what he had not had before and He gave him Paradise in the next life. If that good neighbor had been hateful, he would have conspired against the unbelieving one in order to destroy him. Those who run after this world and forget Him, God makes them chase this world all their life.

God is the Wisest of Judges (*Ahkam ul-hakimin*). This is a description, but in reality no comparison is possible between God and another judge. He alone is the Ultimate Judge, and His Essence is beyond any attribute or description. Whatever He decides is the best; and thus you must accept whatever He plans for you. Accept, submit and surrender to His Will and Judgment. Whatever your brother or sister possesses, God planned and gave it to him or her. If you develop hatred because of that, it means you are not happy with your Lord, and are opposing His Wishes. When God wants something to happen—if He wants a person to be rich, to be kind, to be beautiful, to be handsome, to be generous—you cannot challenge His Will. You cannot hate that person's gifts, for it will take you into a state of unbelief.

Many people do not realize they have this trait. Look at yourself and be truthful. Are you not thinking, "Why is my boss pressuring me? He is not better than me. He's stupid; he doesn't know anything!" or something of that sort? You must not say such things, for you are a servant, and servants obey. You are a Muslim, a believer who must surrender to God's Will.

What does a patient say to the doctor? "Help me! What do you think I have? I will listen to you!" We must all listen to the Best of Physicians, *Ahkam ul-hakimi*.[68] When we do not accept His decisions, is when we begin to develop hatred against others. When a person does not accept, far from being happy and satisfied with God's plans, he instead comes against His plans and begins to find ways to hurt people he sees as receiving "more," achieving "more" or owning "more." Today, we are seeing how much people hurt each other and how innocent people are often killed or thrown into prison. Over the entire globe, the powerful oppress the weak. Those with hatred inside their hearts do not care about living in peace; they want to control everyone and enslave them.

Our duty is to surrender to God's Will. We must say, "O my Lord, you know better. The tyrants are not following Your way, but I leave it up to You to take revenge on them. I am living according to what You are asking of me." Perhaps through the tyrants He is testing us. Perhaps He is cleansing us. Do you think God will harm those who say, "There is no god but God, Muhammad ﷺ is the Messenger of God?" On Judgment Day they will be rewarded for believing in Him, for whoever says "There is no god but God (*la ilaha ill-Allah*)" will enter Paradise,[ix] by God's Mercy and by the intercession of the Prophet. With all the

---

[68] The title *hakim* covers both the judge and the doctor, since its meaning is "wise."

difficulties we now see around the world, God is cleansing Muslims. Thus, we must not fight. Rather, we must surrender. You must learn to say from your heart, "O my Lord, if this is Your Will, I have no hatred in my heart toward anyone. Let them have what they want."

## MOSES' RESPONSE

God commanded Moses ﷺ to speak a gentle word to Pharaoh, and Moses ﷺ did, although Pharaoh did not listen. So, Moses ﷺ left him, and God told him, "Gather the Children of Israel and go!" He did not command Moses ﷺ to fight the unbelievers. God sent the prophets Moses ﷺ and Aaron ﷺ to show Pharaoh that he was wrong. Yet, when Pharaoh rejected the Truth, Moses ﷺ and Aaron ﷺ did not raise the Children of Israel against him.

That is one of the lessons Moses ﷺ taught us through these events, that we must not kill out of hatred—even hatred for an aggressor. Moses ﷺ challenged Pharaoh with knowledge and with faith. His request for Pharaoh to allow the Children of Israel to leave Egypt was rejected. Moses ﷺ responded with a miracle, and even when Pharaoh rejected the miracle, Moses ﷺ did not fight. Pharaoh assembled his magicians to respond to the miracle, claiming it was only magic. They were unable to challenge Moses with their simple tricks, and when they witnessed the reality that Moses ﷺ brought—his staff becoming a snake which swallowed theirs—they all prostrated to God and accepted Moses ﷺ. Moses ﷺ gathered the Children of Israel and left, and it was Pharaoh who was overcome with hatred.

Rebellion and retaliation are derived from the love of this world and the hatred that follows from that infatuation. Pharaoh was driven by his love for the world, which inspired him to hate Moses ﷺ, rebel against the Divine Plan and retaliate. With his entire army he pursued Moses ﷺ, and God told His Prophet ﷺ, "Do not worry. Go to the sea." Moses ﷺ followed this guidance, and when he arrived at the shore of the Red Sea, God spoke to him again, saying, "Strike the water with your staff." When Moses did, that great body of water miraculously became like a tunnel, through which Moses and the Children of Israel passed to the other side, while Pharaoh and everyone with him perished.

Hatred destroys human beings. It is forbidden to show hatred towards anyone. Instead you must say, "O my Lord, for Your sake I hold nothing against anyone."

Once, when his Companions were assembled, the Prophet Muhammad pointed to one of them and said, "He is going to enter Paradise." Sayyidina 'Umar , one of the Prophet's closest Companions, wanted to know what that person was doing to achieve such a station so he could emulate him. Sayyidina 'Umar observed that man keeping the night prayer, and sleeping afterwards. The man did not awaken during the night for supererogatory prayers, although he followed the Prophet in the morning prayer and all the other obligatory prayers—nothing more and nothing less. Sayyidina 'Umar was astonished, so he finally asked that Companion, "The Prophet said that you will enter Paradise, so I sought to know what you are doing so as to be like you. But I am not seeing anything exceptional in your conduct."

The man replied, "Yet there is something I do that is the reason for the Prophet's words." So Sayyidina 'Umar asked, "What is that?" The man answered, "Before I sleep, I forgive everyone who harmed me. I do not allow hatred in my heart towards anyone. When I sleep, I say, 'O my Lord, for your Love and the love of Prophet Muhammad , I forgive everyone.' If God were to give me the entire wealth of this world into my possession, it would not make any difference to me. I am never happy about owning anything, so if I lose it at the end of the day, I am never sad and I have no regrets. I am subject to God's Will, and whatever He wants to do with me, I am accepting."

Hatred thrives on unbelief and disobedience. We must always avoid it, because it increases heedlessness in our hearts. It is a veil that makes us forget that God is the Wisest of the Wise. What God plans for us all, we must accept. We must not object to it. If God gives good to anyone, in this world or the next, we must agree with His Decision. If God made someone a doctor, an engineer, a king or a scholar, we must accept that. If He makes you a janitor, cleaning up after others, you must say, "O my Lord, you made me a janitor, and I am happy with what You have planned for me."

Look at the shoeshine man: his customers come with dirty shoes, and sit on high chairs overlooking everyone, looking down on him. His customers are so happy to sit on those raised chairs, while the shoeshine man sits low, beneath everyone, never complaining. They toss him a tip, and he is satisfied with so little, just a bit of food and enough money to pay for his humble lifestyle. His heart is content.

God gave us all from His Grace, and still we have hatred toward each other. May God forgive us, and make us content with what He gave us and help us to accept His plan.

الحسد

## 4. JEALOUSY (*AL-HASAD*)

The Prophet ﷺ said:

*Do not envy one another, do not hate each other and do not slander one another. Be servants of God, brethren altogether.*[69]

Aspiring to have the same good another possesses is envy, while desiring to see it removed from him is jealousy. Because jealousy is the trunk of a great tree among the negative characteristics, human beings need God to protect them from it.

God revealed to his Prophet ﷺ the Chapter of the Dawn as a protection against jealousy and black magic:

*I seek refuge in the Lord of the Dawn;*
*from the mischief of created things;*

*and from the mischief of darkness as it is overspread;*

*and from the mischief of those who blow on knots;*
*and from the mischief of the envious one as he envies.*[70]

Through this chapter of the Qur'an, God is teaching us to ask, "O God! Give us refuge from every kind of fear and every kind of danger and evil." The appeal begins with, "O God, we seek refuge in You," and continues, "from any mischief that is created, anything that may harm us, any danger." Specifically, this refers

---

[69] Ibn Majah and *Musnad* Ahmad, with additional wording, "and it is not permitted for a Muslim to cut off his brother over three days…"
[70] Suratu 'l-Falaq [Daybreak], 113.

to protection from the mischief of conjurers who recite words, then blow on knots in order to perform black magic on people. You are asking God to protect you from this darkest form of mischief.

Such mischief proceeds from jealousy, the jealousy one person harbors for another. Those people loathe for others to receive God's favors. They do not want anything of goodness for others, but prefer everything for themselves.

Hatred is different. When a hateful person sees that someone has something they want, that person makes a conspiracy to possess it or to deprive the other of it. With jealousy, a person wants everything and cannot accept anyone having anything. They do not want others to experience goodness or to be happy, and so they try to destroy others.

An example of this is the cause of the first murder when Cain killed Abel as related in the Holy Qur'an:

> Recite to them the truth of the story of the two sons of
> Adam ﷺ. Behold! they each presented a sacrifice (to
> God): It was accepted from one, but not from the other.[71]

Jealousy and bitter rivalry had grown in Cain's heart, particularly after his brother Abel was given the more beautiful of two sisters in marriage, and the "last straw" was God's rejection of his sacrifice.[x] The Qur'an relates:

> Said the latter [Cain]: "Be sure I will slay you."
> "Surely," said the former [Abel], "(God) does accept of
> the sacrifice of those who are righteous. If you do stretch
> your hand against me, to slay me, it is not for me to
> stretch my hand against you to slay you: for I do fear
> God, the Cherisher of the worlds."[72]

Beyond physical violence, the worst way to destroy humanity is through black magic.

---

[71] Suratu 'l-Ma'ida [The Spread Table], 5:27.
[72] Suratu 'l-Ma'ida, 5:28.

The Holy Qur'an mentions two angels,[73] Harut and Marut, who visited this world and stayed because they liked it so much, causing God's curse to fall on them. It is from these two that the art of black magic derives. To this day, its practice is thriving in the Caribbean, throughout Africa, the Indian sub-continent and the Far East.

Some naively assert it is harmful only if one believes in it. However, refusing to acknowledge a danger in no way confers immunity or protection from magic any more than it does from a tornado.

This dark power has a very devastating effect on people, whether they recognize it or not. You cannot simply say it can only work if you believe in it. Why would God reveal verses of protection from black magic if it did not exist?

Some practitioners of this dark art tried to perform black magic on Prophet Muhammad ﷺ. This was the cause for the revelation of the Chapter of the Daybreak, for although the Prophet ﷺ was divinely protected, God wanted us to learn about this dark practice, to be aware of it, to be protected from it and to guard against it. The casting of spells by means of knots tied in ropes was a favorite form of witchcraft practiced by perverted women at that time. Such secret arts cause psychological terror. Their practitioners display seductive charms and spread false rumors that slander the innocent, and deter their victims from taking corrective action. It was for this reason that God revealed that chapter and said, "O Muhammad ﷺ, recite *'and from the mischief of those who blow on knots'* and blow on thyself." So the Prophet ﷺ recited and blew on himself until all that black magic was dispelled.

God is showing us that, although it did not affect the Prophet ﷺ, black magic can affect us. Historical research proves that not only are there many ways to carry out black magic through

---

[73] Suratu 'l-Baqara [The Cow], 2:96.

various practices and applications, but also that this dark art has prevailed in all the world's various cultures until today. Some forms make use of the unseen beings known as genies (*jinn*) and demons (*shayatin*).

## EXORCISM

I was visiting a group of students some years ago, and they brought a woman to me who was an observant, practicing Muslim. However, they feared that someone had targeted her with black magic. She spoke French and no Arabic, yet she would go out of control and begin speaking and cursing in fluent classical Arabic, even going so far as to blaspheme against God and the Prophet ﷺ, and repeating, "I am not Muslim!" over and over. At other times she would scream, "There is no God!" The sounds she made were not human, and at times her body was violently out of her control.

May God bless our masters, Mawlana Shaykh Nazim ق and Grandshaykh 'Abd Allah ق, who taught us what to recite in such situations to repel the evil spirits that possess people. Not everything you recite will necessarily cure the patient, and what you must recite varies from one case to another. I recited what my shaykhs guided me to recite at that time, following their instruction. As I recited, the genie possessing that woman, a demon, repeated back to me whatever I recited. Then I shouted, and the genie shouted back. Everyone present became very afraid, as I reached a level in the recitation where either the genie would be cast out of her body, or it would burn me. At that moment, Shaykh Nazim ق appeared to me spiritually and instructed, "Recite such-and-such prayer." I recited what Shaykh Nazim ق instructed me to say and the genie was suddenly defeated. The woman returned to her senses, and the genie left her body through her big toe.

Islamic history is rich with such accounts[74], providing documented cases of and instructions for curing specific illnesses. For example, if you want to cure some kinds of maladies, these traditions indicate you must enter into seclusion for five days during the full moon, specifically the thirteenth through the seventeenth of the lunar calendar. Specific supplications must be recited and specific acts must be performed that are designed to relieve that affliction so the patient may be cured. This is a science that has been handed down over the centuries, and it includes protection against the evil eye and black magic.

We are examining these details at length here, because we must understand the cause of black magic, why it exists and how it has been sustained for so long. We must understand that it is serious enough and real enough that God revealed an entire chapter of the Qur'an to address this issue. Moreover, it is important to understand that black magic is generated and sustained by jealousy. Those who practice this dark art do not want others to have anything. They do not like the Prophet ﷺ to have prophethood; they do not like someone beautiful to possess beauty, someone wealthy to enjoy his wealth nor someone blessed with a skill to benefit from it. Jealousy and envy are very powerful states that may affect any of us. It is for this that we recite the last verse of the Qur'an's Daybreak chapter, *"and from the mischief of the envious one as he practices envy."* [75]

The one who is envious, whose heart is filled with jealousy, will work to destroy you, perhaps even to kill you. For this reason it is important not to tell people everything that you do and what bounties you receive, for then jealousy will be directed toward you. Jealous people cannot accept that you are in a good situation instead of them. They do not like you to benefit and do well. Remember, malignant envy translated into action seeks to destroy

---

[74] The late Shaykh Metwalli Sha'rawi of Egypt related many such contemporary accounts in his books and lectures.
[75] Suratu 'l-Falaq [Daybreak], 113:5.

the material or spiritual happiness enjoyed by others. The best defense against it is to always trust in God with purity of heart.

This warning does not contradict the verse, *"And as for the Bounty of your Lord, proclaim (it)."*[76] God allowed jealousy to exist in some hearts, to teach us to follow His Way and not the way of Satan. Anyone who follows God's Way will never become envious of others; this is a characteristic reserved exclusively for followers of Satan. However, the Prophet ﷺ encouraged competition among the Companions in good deeds and worship, to inspire them and others to goodness. To be envious of someone who prayed 500 cycles of prayer, or who gave a large sum in charity or opened a mosque, is permissible as these are acts that inspire goodness and piety. They are acts for which we should all strive. That is competition for goodness, and it is acceptable. But jealousy that seeks to prevent good coming to others, is not acceptable. That sort of jealousy is a sickness that can only worsen until it destroys the person afflicted by it. Such people will envy anyone, even their own parents, children or spouse, sometimes even their very own selves.

The Prophet ﷺ said:

*Jealousy consumes good deeds just as fire consumes wood.*[77]

According to Grandshaykh 'Abd Allah ق, the way to eliminate jealousy is to observe the voluntary Prayer of Salvation (Salat an-Najat). This is made before the morning prayer (Salat al-Fajr) and after the prayer for ablution (Salat tahiyat al-wudu). At its conclusion, prostration is made and the following is recited: "O my Lord! Jealousy is consuming my good deeds like fire burns wood, so remove it from me."

Jealousy devours good deeds by creating bad intentions towards others, causing the jealous one to plot against those who

---

[76] Suratu 'd-Duha [Forenoon], 93:11.

[77] Abu Dawud, Ibn Majah with additional wording "and charity extinguishes sins like water extinguishes flame; prayer is the light of a believer and fasting his protection from the Fire.

have something more. Such discontent is, in reality, a challenge to God, Who is ultimately the Source of all blessings. Sometimes, despite ourselves, bad thoughts come into our hearts. Perhaps, when you learn that someone has received a large sum of money, you think, "How did he get that money? Here I am, working so hard, struggling in two jobs, and it came to him!" At such a time it is better to remember that the Best of Planners is God. It is better to think, "My Lord wants that person to have that money. God knows what I need and will give me what I need, so I am happy. All praises are due to God. Even if He does not give me what I asked for, I must be happy. I must accept God's decision."

We are sinners. We are struggling. Do not say, "I have no jealousy." All of us are inflicted with it. If we are aware of it and struggle against it, then we will be safe. However, to surrender to it only makes jealousy grow stronger.

We say, "May God blind the jealous eye," for if the jealous person could not see, he or she would be cured of this disease. A great burden of jealousy is that God causes the jealous one go to the grave with it. Thus, it is destructive in this life and in the next. May God protect us.

العجب

## 5. VANITY (AL-'UJB)

*God loves not the proud.*[78]

In a Sacred Tradition God says:

*Pride is My cloak and Greatness is My covering. Whoever competes with Me regarding them, I shall cast them into the Hellfire.*[79]

Vanity is a very dangerous attribute. Today, children are constantly taught, "Be proud of yourself." Someone who is proud sees himself or herself as the strongest, the prettiest, the smartest, the fastest, the best. They think they can achieve what no one else can. This teaching instills in children a sense of unbridled independence, encouraging a belief that they know more and everyone around them knows less. It also prompts them to reject advice, as they are told that their own thinking is sufficient and superior.

It is also common today to hear parents praising their children by saying, "I am so proud of you." You may say, "I'm happy with you," but using the world "proud" teaches the child vanity, to see himself or herself as the better than everyone else. It breeds conceit and arrogance in the child, as well as in the "proud" parents. This thinking also leads children to reject their parents later in life, to see them as ignorant, backwards, old-fashioned and

---

[78] Suratu 'n-Nahl [The Bee], 16:23.
[79] Abu Dawud.

awkward. Instead of thinking, "I am proud of my father because he raised me," they think in accordance with what was instilled in them in childhood: "I am proud of *myself.*"

## JIHAD OF THE INNER SELF

Returning from a military campaign against aggressors who sought to exterminate the community of believers, the Prophet ﷺ said to his Companions:

*We come from the lesser struggle (jihad) and are facing the greater struggle.*[80]

He meant that, while they had struggled against enemy aggressors, they were still faced with the challenge of fighting the lower ways of the inner self. The ego always wants to be on top. It cannot accept to be low. One must cut down vanity and make the inner-self prostrate, for one who truly submits to his Lord can no longer submit to his self. Once that state is reached, prayer is purely for God. For this reason the Prophet ﷺ said:

*What I fear most for my Community is the hidden polytheism.*[81]

He feared for his community not the outward polytheism of idol-worship, for he was informed by God that his community was protected from that, forever,[xi] but the secret polytheism, which is to do something for the sake of showing-off. The Prophet ﷺ could never associate anyone with God, for he is God's most perfect servant. Nonetheless he was told to say:

*I am but a man like yourselves, but the inspiration has come to me that your God is One ...*[82]

The Prophet ﷺ showed his simplicity and humility by saying, "I am a human being like you, but God is sending His revelation

---

[80] Al-Khatib al-Baghdadi, al-Bayhaqi, al-Ghazali.

[81] Al-Hakim in *al-Mustadrak* (authentic). In a similar vein, the Prophet is reported to have said, "Association with God (*shirk*) is stealthier in this community than creeping ants."

[82] Suratu 'l-Kahf [The Cave], 18:110.

to me." Although the Prophet ﷺ remains always—then and now—in God's Presence, even in this unequaled privilege he is utterly humble and devoid of arrogance, considering himself "like you," when that expression included all human beings. One sees in this exactly the opposite of vanity, for the Prophet ﷺ sought to find any means of coming closer to people, in order to make them familiar and eventually open their hearts to the truth.

Contemporary scholars of the Wahhabi sect of Islam have erroneously interpreted this statement to mean, "He is a human being like us." Quite to the contrary, Imam Suyuti's explanation of this verse is that it was revealed to the Prophet ﷺ in the context of the verse preceding it, affirming that if all the oceans of the universes became ink, and all the trees became pens and those pens used all that ink to write, never could all the Words of God be written. In that incomparable knowledge in which God put his beloved Prophet ﷺ, the Prophet ﷺ compared himself to that Greatness and said, "O my Lord, I am only a human being." His claim is relative to that Greatness, not to other human beings. The Prophet ﷺ is describing himself as a human being out of fear and awe of being in God's Presence. Thus, he cannot say, "I am something." So he humbled himself.

If the Prophet ﷺ, who in reality is the only one who has a right to have pride, the one whom God raised up to His Own Presence on the Night Journey and Ascension, was not proud, why are people proud of themselves today? Who gave them the authority to teach their children to be proud?

We should never associate good deeds with ourselves, for if not for God's favor, we would not have been able to do them, as He said in the Holy Qur'an:

> But God has created you and what ye do![83]

So do not be proud of yourself. May God forgive us.

---

[83] Suratu 's-Saffat [The Rangers], 37:96.

## 6. STINGINESS (AL-BUKHL)

*And those saved from the covetousness of their souls,*
*they are the ones who achieve prosperity.*[84]

The Prophet ﷺ said:

> *The one who is open-handed is close to God, to mankind and to*
> *Paradise, and remote from Hellfire. The miser is remote from*
> *God, from mankind and from Paradise, and close to Hellfire. A*
> *generous ignoramus is more beloved to God than a stingy*
> *worshipper.*[85]

The Prophet Muhammad ﷺ encouraged us to have good manners and to follow his footsteps. About His Beloved Prophet ﷺ, God said:

> *Certainly you are of a tremendous character.*[86]

In this statement, God is describing his Prophet ﷺ, and in this case the word "tremendous" means "without limit." The good characteristics of the Prophet ﷺ cannot be adequately described because they are limitless. We are unable to describe what God has given to His Prophet. With the example of his tremendous

---

[84] Suratu 'l-Hashr [The Gathering], 59: 9.
[85] Tirmidhi.
[86] Suratu 'l-Qalam [The Pen], 68:4. "Tremendous character" in Arabic: *khuluqin*
*'adheem.*

character, the Prophet ﷺ wants his Community to leave bad characteristics and follow his footsteps.

People can exemplify stinginess in many different ways, even as simply as in withholding a smile.

The Prophet ﷺ said:

*To make someone happy is from faith.*[87]

If you have the ability to make people happy, do so. If you keep this ability, this power to yourself, you are stingy.

Stinginess is a characteristic of Satan. With his jealousy and anger, Satan questioned the creation of human beings. When God commanded him to prostrate to Adam ﷺ, Satan refused because of his stinginess. He saw himself as great. He did not want anyone other than himself to benefit, and so did not want Adam ﷺ to remain in Paradise. Satan conspired against him to cut off the honor Adam ﷺ was receiving.

God is generous. He said that for each good deed He credits us for ten good deeds.[88] For one prayer made in the Friday congregation He gives credit for twenty-seven.[89] Do not be stingy; "A stingy person is an enemy of God, and a generous person is the beloved of God."

The Prophet ﷺ said:

*Even to remove something harmful from the street is from faith.*[90]

If removing something harmful from the way of human beings is from faith, then to ignore the harm that may befall others is an act of stinginess. If you have no faith, you are going to be stingy; indeed, you are going to dress yourself in every one of the ruinous traits.

---

[87] At-Tabarani.

[88] As narrated in a Prophetic Tradition from Ibn 'Abbas, in Bukhari and Muslim.

[89] The Messenger of God ﷺ said, "Prayer in congregation is twenty-seven times more meritorious than a prayer performed individually." Bukhari and Muslim.

[90] Bukhari and Muslim.

## GENEROSITY OF MUSLIMS

The Prophet ﷺ said:

*The stingy person is one who, when my name is mentioned, does not invoke blessings on me.*[91]

The Prophet ﷺ is not stingy. For every prayer you send on him, he sends you ten in fulfillment of his promise:

*Whoever prays upon me, God will pray upon him ten times.*[92]

How many times people say "Muhammad ﷺ, Muhammad" without respect, as if they are speaking about their friend or colleague at school! Imam Shafi'i never said, "Muhammad" without saying, "Prophet ﷺ Muhammad." In the ritual prayer, some Schools of Law recite: "O God, bless Muhammad ﷺ and his Family, as you have blessed Abraham and his Family." Imam Shafi'i disputed this practice and taught his students to always attach the title "Sayyidina" "our Master," to the name of the Prophet ﷺ, "O God, bless Sayyidina Muhammad and his Family, as you have blessed Sayyidina Abraham and his Family." This is how Imam Shafi'i kept respect for the Master. What could be the objection to adding "Sayyidina" to the recitation? Its utterance is nothing but an expression of generosity.

During Ottoman rule, whenever the Prophet's name was mentioned in the Imperial Court, the sultan and everyone in attendance stood up, out of respect. Today, everyone stands for rulers, yet they sit when the Prophet ﷺ is mentioned.

We have bad characteristics that we cannot see. Every moment that passes without our tongues being moist in the Remembrance of God, we are stingy.

*Someone came to the Prophet ﷺ and asked, "O Messenger of God, I am finding that all these different rules of the religion are too*

---

[91] *Kanz al-'Ummal.*
[92] Ibn Abi Shaybah, Ahmad, 'Abd bin Hamid and at-Tirmidhi.

*difficult. Please give me something easy that I may accomplish."* The Prophet ﷺ answered, *"Make your tongue moist with the Remembrance of God."*[93]

God is teaching us, "Do not be stingy in remembering Me, O My servant."

When the rites of the Pilgrimage are nearing completion, God specifically instructs pilgrims in the Qur'an:

> *Celebrate the praises of God, as ye used to celebrate the praises of your fathers—yea, with far more heart and soul.*[94]

Children call on their parents whenever they encounter problems. God reminds us that we must call on Him even more than we would call on our own parents. Failing to remember God and call on Him is also stinginess. We must keep in mind the example of *"Those who remember God, sitting or standing or lying down."*[95] The lesson is not to allow yourself to be stingy at any moment of your life. Look how generous God is in all that He gives us! Going back to the earlier example of the wrestler, even when we throw something at a fruit tree and damage it, what does it give back except fruit? They are not stingy. The saints are like fruit trees; although people harm them, they give back rewards.

Grandshaykh 'Abd Allah ق narrated a classic example of how generous the saints are. When Sayyidina Bayazid al-Bistami ق was attacked by the people of his village, he asked God, "O my Lord, open Your door for me." A reply was then revealed to him spiritually: "O Bayazid, you must first become a garbage dump for My servants. To achieve that level, you must carry the burdens of My Creation." Sayyidina Bayazid al-Bistami ق then returned to his people and became a dump for them, carrying all their pain

---

[93] Ahmad, Tirmidhi, Ibn Majah, and Ibn Hibban (*hasan*).
[94] Suratu 'l-Baqara [The Cow], 2:200.
[95] Surat Ali-'Imran [Family of 'Imran], 3:191.

and suffering. They even threw stones at him until he fell unconscious, and when they were certain he was dead, they carried his body and tossed it upon a heap of garbage.

When Sayyidina Bayazid ق regained consciousness, he prayed, "O my Lord, those who harm me, forgive them and send them to Paradise. I wish that I would die and have You create me again, so that they may again harm me and I may again ask for their forgiveness. Then let them kill me. I will carry their pain, suffering and burdens, and You can forgive them again." God replied, "Whoever forgives and makes peace, God rewards them. For your sake, I am forgiving everyone and making peace."

Stinginess means refusing to let go of anything, and thus always leads to greed. The most stingy of people are those who seek to prevent others from attaining God's mercy. They say, "They are going to hell, because of this and that which they used to do." What does God say?

> *"Behold! are these not the men whom you swore that God with His Mercy would never bless? Enter ye the Garden: no fear shall be on you, nor shall ye grieve."*[96]

May God protect us.

---

[96] Suratu 'l-'Araf [The Heights], 7:49.

## 7. AVARICE (*AL-TAMA'*)

*To whom I made (life) smooth and comfortable! Yet he desires that I should add (yet more).*[97]

The Prophet 鸒 said:

*Avarice removes wisdom from the hearts of the scholars.*[98]

Avarice is another vice, defined as having one's eye on what others own and having no limit to hoarding one's own possessions. If you have everything and your neighbor has nothing, you must covet his nothing to add to your everything. Greed is the essence of all problems, making it so that your eyes are never satisfied. You are not seeing God before you; you are only seeing how you can grab a larger piece of this world. If you see something nice you want it. Your eyes are never full.

As an example, imagine that you are attending a dinner. The host serves so many dishes, and of course he cannot place all of them in front of you. The greedy person is the one whose eyes are focused on the dish at the other end of the table, far beyond his reach. In fact, he is not satisfied until he gets a portion from that dish, no matter whom he inconveniences or troubles.

When Adam 鸒 came on earth, God wanted to test him. He sent Archangel Gabriel 鸒 to earth in the form of a man. And Adam 鸒 said, "Are you also living here on this planet?" "Yes," the

---

[97] Suratu 'l-Muddaththir [The Enveloped One], 74:14, 15.
[98] As-Suyuti, who graded it authentic.

angel replied, "Are you are living here?" Adam 🕮 answered, "Yes. I am, therefore we must divide the earth between us." Gabriel 🕮 said, "You take half and I will take half." Adam 🕮 said, "No, you are one person, while we are two. Eve and I. Therefore you take one-third and I will take two-thirds." Gabriel 🕮 said, "No, I will take half and you take half. I do not care how many you are."

Adam 🕮 said, "No, I must take two-thirds." Gabriel 🕮 refused and Adam 🕮 insisted. Finally they began to fight. Gabriel 🕮 being stronger put Adam 🕮 down. Then he took a stick and drew a line, and said, "This is my side and that is your side." Later Gabriel 🕮 said, "The wind and water might erase it. Let us set up stones to mark it." They placed a big stone as a marker between the two "territories." But Adam 🕮 did not like it. He said, "That stone is a little bit more on my side. It must be a little more on your side. Gabriel 🕮 said, "No, it is correct." Adam 🕮 said, "It must be moved." Gabriel 🕮 said, "No, it is right." And they began to fight again and Gabriel 🕮 put Adam 🕮 down again. But even as he held Adam 🕮 down, preventing him from reaching the stone, Adam 🕮 stretched out his foot in order to push the stone with it and increase his territory.

Half the world and they wanted more. Today they are putting up borders on every country. The Holy Qur'an says:

*Spacious is God's earth!* [99]

There were no borders 200 years ago. People could go wherever you wanted. They would move and migrate without hindrance. You were able to travel to Muslim countries, just as you were able to go to Europe, Africa and America. At that time there were no borders, no visas and no restrictions on what to bring and take out. That is why they have erected borders today — learning from Adam 🕮 and Gabriel 🕮.

---

[99] Suratu 'z-Zumar [The Groups], 39:10.

For that reason the Sufis say, "Nothing fills the greedy eye of man but dust," meaning one's desires will never be satisfied, no matter how much one acquires, until filled by the dust of the grave. God says:

> *And let not those who covetously withhold of the gifts which God Has given them of His Grace, think that it is good for them: Nay, it will be the worse for them: soon shall the things which they covetously withheld be tied to their necks like a twisted collar, on the Day of Judgment. To God belongs the heritage of the heavens and the earth; and God is well-acquainted with all that ye do.*[100]

---

[100] Surat Ali-'Imran [The Family of 'Imran], 3:180.

## 8. COWARDICE (*AL-JUBN*)

People are always putting their will before God's Will. God's Will comes first, then our will. What God wants from us, we have to do. If we are not doing it, that means we are putting our ego between us and our Lord.

What is a coward? A coward is someone that runs away from difficult situations. His personality is weak, so he runs away from difficulties. The opposite of cowardice is bravery.

Cowardice is one of the seventeen characteristics that are not accepted by gnostics on their journey to God's Presence. That journey to the Divine Presence is the path trod by the seekers of the spiritual way that the saints of God traversed, imitating the prophets and messengers of God. That means imitating them as well, in the difficulties they carried.

Look how the Prophet Jonah ﷺ faced the difficulties before him when the whale swallowed him. Look at Zachariah ﷺ, father of the Prophet John ﷺ. When the people were chasing him to kill him, God caused a tree to open up, and he entered inside it. Seeing that, the people came and sawed the tree in half in order to cut him to pieces. He held out under this terrible penalty. All the Prophets of God were brave in the face of difficulties.

*The Prophet Muhammad ﷺ said, "Not one prophet carried what I carried of difficulties."*[101]

---

[101] Imam adh-Dhahabi in his *Tarikh al-Islam.*

Pious people must follow the footsteps of the Prophet ﷺ by being brave. The Prophet ﷺ stood up by himself alone, calling to God without any support. That required great courage and bravery, the opposite of cowardice.

The saints of God, both those who passed away and those who are living, are always brave against the four enemies of human beings: the ego (*nafs*), worldly desires (*dunya*), lust (*hawa*) and Satan.

When you follow your low desires, your ego becomes very happy. These desires are related to the things of this world and this life. When you fall in love with something that is worldly, you are turning away from God's beautiful Names and Attributes, running towards something that at some time is going to disintegrate into dust. That is what we call bad desires, the desires of our lower nature. All of these lead to the highest level of evil: Satan. Those are the four enemies of human beings: Ego, worldly desires, lust and Satan. Cowardice makes you run away from facing the difficulty of stepping on these four. Whoever opposes them, will be considered brave in the Divine Presence.

Why was Sayyidina 'Ali ؓ called Asadullah al-Ghalib, the Victorious Lion of God? It is because he stepped on his devil. He was not a coward. He was brave, able to move.

Why was Sayyidina Abu Bakr as-Siddiq ؓ called as-Siddiq, the Veracious? Because he was brave. *Sidq*, veracity, comes from firmness of belief. He believed in everything that the Prophet ﷺ said. He stepped on his doubts and on Satan's gossiping in his ears. His attention was only on the Prophet. He only listened for what the Prophet Muhammad ﷺ was going to say, so that he could hear it and do it.

Sayyidina 'Umar ؓ was called "al-Faruq." Al-Faruq is the one who has separated truth (*haqq*) from falsehood (*batil*). He put falsehood down. He was brave. He was not a coward. He did not let cowardice take him. Sayyidina 'Umar ؓ was believing, then separating falsehood from truth, bringing truth and reality up and putting falsehood down.

The third caliph, Sayyidina 'Uthman Dhu 'n-Nurayn ☀, was not a coward either, particularly when it came to giving. People today have become cowards in giving, so that when someone asks something from them—a donation or charity—their hands shake. Sayyidina 'Uthman ☀ gave and gave and kept giving, and his hand never shook.

It is cowardice which is causing us to be lost in the darkness of this transient, worldly life. That is why it is a harmful trait which we must eliminate from our lives. Everything we see before us leads to cowardice, because we are not brave enough to face the opposition of our four personal enemies.

If you go through a red light without stopping, what happens? You are ticketed and fined. There are red lights in every person's life that he or she must not cross. However, due to our weak character and cowardice, we are crossing these red lights. Indeed, we all know how many red lights we are running and how many tickets we are receiving. Satan has conquered us for we are not defying him nor repelling his advances. Therefore, on Judgment Day, God is going to give us our tickets—and there will be many, despite the fact that God is Generous and does not multiply our faults as He does our good deeds.

Sins are not multiplied. One sin is only recorded as one bad deed by our attending angel scribes. Yet, good deeds are multiplied. When you pray, fast or give charity, it is rewarded many times over, for God is Most Generous with what He is giving. In this world, if you do not pay your fines on time, the judge may increase your penalty many times over. You may even go to jail. God is giving us time to pay our fines and repent. However, He is telling us not to be cowardly; not to follow Satan.

To prevent that cowardice from overcoming our hearts we must keep our hearts always awake through the remembrance of God. When you remember God, you are always awake, on guard. What is the strongest protection from Satan? Satan is afraid to approach a believer. By keeping your heart in constant remembrance of God, Satan cannot approach you, for he cannot approach someone who has full protection.

What must one do to achieve full protection? One must always maintain one's ablution (*wudu*). Whenever you lose it, renew it and go and perform two cycles of prayer. Then you are protected from Satan. That is the first shield to protect you from Satan's traps. The second is to keep your heart awake by remembering God. When you do, satisfaction comes to the heart. God said:

> *Verily, by God's remembrance, satisfaction, peace,*
> *calmness and tranquility will enter the heart.*[102]

The pavement of your heart, therefore, must become the remembrance of God.

One person was asked, "Why do you sleep so much?" He answered, "The sleep of an oppressor is worship." That man saw he was oppressing the soul that God gave him, for he was not fulfilling its rights. So he slept. When one is sleeping, it is as if one is in a coma. When you sleep you are "out," so Satan does not approach you. Moreover, when you go to sleep with ablution and after praying two cycles, you are written in the Divine Presence as one who is in constant prayer. So you wake up for the morning prayer, then go back to sleep. You wake up and pray mid-morning prayer, then sleep; pray the noon prayer, then sleep; pray the afternoon prayer, then sleep; pray sunset prayer, then sleep and so on. What this means in metaphor is, make your ego sleep from desire for this world.

The saints of God know they are not brave enough to face their egos; they know that they would oppress themselves if they allowed their selves to have their way. So they sleep. That means they submit to God's Will, sleeping in the Divine Presence. That is submission. When someone sleeps, he is in complete submission, not even moving. That is why it is said in Prophetic Tradition that as soon as someone sleeps, after having made ablution, nine parts

---

[102] Suratu 'r-Ra'd [Thunder], 13:28.

out of his soul's ten parts are taken out of his body. That soul will be making prostration under the Throne of the Merciful ('*Arshu 'r-Rahman*).

When someone is submitting, remembering he is an oppressor to himself, praying two cycles and sleeping, thus letting God's Will override his own will, God makes his soul to come under the Throne and go into prostration (*sajda*). In contrast, those who are spending their nights and days entertaining their egos find no time for God's worship. That is because God's worship is the most difficult burden on the self. For that reason, people are not brave enough to stop what they are doing and move towards the Divine Presence.

O believers, O spiritual people, you are the light of this universe. You who are spiritually enlightened, seeking reality and looking for the truth, working hard to progress, do not let cowardice enter into your life. It is one of the worst of the rejected characteristics. That cowardice is something Satan is throwing into our hearts. May God take that cowardice from us and make us to move towards the Divine Presence, to be brave in the face of life's difficulties and seek out the best outcome.

البطالة

## 9. INDOLENCE (*AL-BATALAH*)

The Prophet ﷺ said:

*The worst thing in the world is inactivity.*[103]

And he ﷺ said:

*I dislike a man who is useless. He is neither engaged in any worldly activity nor any activity for the afterlife.*[104]

A high level of unemployment, or inactivity, in society leads to economic recession. In a recession, the ability to sustain a good quality of life throughout the community is reduced. The economy may even collapse. It is the same with human beings. As soon as we become lazy and cease to follow the Path of the Prophet ﷺ, the quality of our lives diminishes.

We must not allow ourselves to become inactive. We are servants; God has employed us all:

> *Verily I have created jinn and man, only to worship Me.*[105]

God's mercy encompasses those who stay firm on the Path, saying their prayers, fasting, giving charity and performing the Pilgrimage. Those who become inactive leave the Path that God has defined for them. We must follow what God wants us to do,

---

[103] Prophetic Tradition.
[104] Bayhaqi, Ahmad.
[105] Suratu 'dh-Dhariyat [The Winnowing Winds], 51:56.

otherwise we will become like Satan, directed towards disbelief (*thumma kafaru*). God directed us towards faith (*thumma amanu*) and said, "You are a faithful servant. Do not be inactive. Do not leave My work for that of Satan." Satan said, *"I will lead all of them astray."*[106] He began with the Prophet Adam ﷺ, but he was not able to reach Prophet Muhammad ﷺ.

Inactivity is when Muslims leave employment in the path of the Prophet Muhammad ﷺ. Unemployment from Islam leads to employment with Satan. Inactivity leads to following wrong desires, because one is turning away from those good practices that help keep the ego under control. We must be gainfully employed in the building of our next life. Then God will strengthen us, according to the verse:

> *God changes not the bad circumstances of a people until they change themselves toward Him.*[107]

This challenges us not to be inactive, but to follow what God commanded and what His Prophet ﷺ exemplified.

## THE PRIMORDIAL PLEDGE OF EMPLOYMENT

The Prophet ﷺ taught us the way to be a good servant, a good employee, when he said, *"If you truly love God, follow me; God will love you."*[108]

The Prophet ﷺ exhibited the perfect balance of life on the Path of Islam: community building, government structure, religious life, social life, economic growth and more. We are employed to work on all these things. We are subjects. When we recited the Testimony of Faith, we accepted to work in accordance with that pledge, not to be inactive. That pledge was witnessed by the Prophet ﷺ and two angels. On Judgment Day, God presents all these agreements and contracts, saying, "My servant made an

---

[106] Suratu 'l-Hijr [The Rocky Tract], 15:39.
[107] Suratu 'r-R'ad [Thunder], 13:11.
[108] Suratu 'n-Nisa [Women], 3:31.

agreement with me. He affirmed the Testimony of Faith, so send him to Paradise. My Mercy will be on those who kept their agreement." For those who made that agreement and were working to fulfill it, God will give them higher and higher rewards. He will raise them to become officers, managers, directors, executive directors and chairmen. God raises them from one Paradise to another. They respected the Employer and lived as employees of the foundation, which is Islam.

Inactivity is spiritual unemployment, a state wherein we are not truly responding to our Employer, to our Creator. People get fired from their jobs if they are not performing up to the standards of the company. However, God promises us, "I will not fire you. You are with Me. But follow My instructions."

Do not waste your time in frivolous pursuits, endlessly going to shopping malls, and movie theaters and playing computer games. Do not waste your time following Satan to indulge in bad desires. Go out to fulfill your necessities or take your family out for some entertainment, but do not exceed the limits of the Path.

Keep remembering God in your leisure time, reciting on your rosary, "There is no God but God (*la ilaha ill-Allah*)." Remember God with every breath. Remember that He gave you that breath with His power and His energy. When you inhale, say *la ilaha ill-Allah*; when you exhale, say *la ilaha ill-Allah*. This is to remember God in every moment, which is the opposite of being inactive. God gave you employment; fulfill it by worshiping Him.

## 10. ARROGANCE (*AL-KIBR*)

*Evil indeed shall be the abode of all given to arrogance.*[109]

The Prophet Noah ﷺ said to his son:

> Do not enter the grave and have in your heart any quantity of arrogance. Arrogance is the dressing of God, and he who competes with Him, God is angry with him.[110]

In the time of the Prophet ﷺ, a group of people known as the People of the Bench, *Ahl as-Suffah*, used to sit morning and evening behind the house of Prophet ﷺ reciting Qur'an, remembering God and praising the Prophet ﷺ. 'Abd Allah ibn Mas'ud related:

> A group from among the Quraysh passed by the Messenger of God ﷺ while Suhayb, Bilal, Ammar, Khabab ؓ and other poor Muslims were with him. They said to the Prophet ﷺ, "O Messenger of God ﷺ, have you chosen this class of people from among your entire followers for your closest ones? Do you want us to follow such people? Are these the ones whom God has chosen from among all of us for His utmost favors? Get rid of them and perhaps if you do that we may follow you.
> It is then that God revealed:

---

[109] Suratu 'n-Nahl [The Bee], 16:29.
[110] Prophetic Tradition.

*Send not away (O Muhammad), those who call on their
Lord morning and evening, seeking His face. In naught
are you accountable for them, and in naught are they
accountable for you, that you should turn them away,
and thus be (one) of the unjust. Thus did We try some of
them by comparison with others, that they should say:
'Is it these then that God has favored from among us?'
Does not God know best those who are grateful?* [111]

Arrogance is to regard oneself higher than others. Those with
arrogance do not like to sit with those of a lower class, for they see
themselves as elite. They desire to only associate and be seen with
other members of high society and shun everyone else. They give
invitations with the stipulation to "Come in formal attire."

God never told us to approach Him in formal dress. He says,
"Come in formal *inner* dress, with your simplicity. Come to Me,
My servant, with humility. Do not be full of arrogance
(*mutakabbir*). Even if you have the highest title in this world, it is
nothing. I am the One Who Gives Titles."

God gave heavenly titles to Prophet Muhammad ﷺ, to all
prophets, to the Companions and to whomever He likes.
Heavenly titles from God have immense value and significance,
whereas worldly titles do not. Even titles such as lord, lady,
knight and dame mean nothing to God. Honor, respect and
dignity are for believers, but supremacy and superiority are only
for God. No one else may be al-Mutakabbir, The Imperious.

The Prophet Muhammad ﷺ went on the Night Journey and
Ascension into the presence of God, closer than any human being
has ever reached in the Divine Presence. When he returned, he
never boasted or tried to exalt himself; he only said, "O my Lord, I
am Your servant ('abd-Allah)!" He was happy to be known as
Servant.

---

[111] Suratu 'l-Ma'idah [The Spread Table], 6:52-53.

*Praise be to God who took His servant to His
Presence.*[112]

The Prophet ﷺ said, "The best moment in all my life, from
beginning to end, is when God called me Servant!" In Arabic the
term *'abd* means to be more than a servant. Its literal meaning is
"slave." So we find in this superb example of humility that the
Prophet ﷺ is happiest to be a slave of God.

Do not think you are something—you are nothing! We must
not have arrogance in ourselves. Iblees had such arrogance when
he protested to God, "But You created him from clay, from dirt.
You created me from energy, from fire. I am better than him. I'm
not going to prostrate to him!" And so God cursed him. Anyone
who has an atom of arrogance in his heart, God will curse him. If
God curses us, immediately we will say, "O Lord, forgive us!"
because we are believers and not like Iblees. We ask God to keep
us informed, that we may repent after every sin we commit. We
commit sins when arrogance veils us from our Lord. Arrogance is
at the root of every sin.

Reflect on the story of the Prophet Joseph ﷺ as narrated in the
Qur'an.[113] He was, according to all accounts, of legendary beauty.
The lady Zulaykha desired him and tried her best to arouse his
carnal desire, tearing at his shirt, inviting him to fornication. Had
Joseph seen himself as the most handsome of men, for that he
was, and if he had been arrogant, he would have been veiled from
his Lord and fallen into sin. Instead, he thought, "God is seeing
me." Then he prayed, *"O God, if You do not protect me I will fall."*[114]
He remembered that the Greatest is God, and that God is
observing all things.

Arrogance blinds us to anyone above us. People who have
arrogance see themselves as the highest, the best, the smartest and

[112] Suratu 'l-Isra [The Night Journey], 17:1.
[113] Surah Yusuf [Joseph], 12:22-34.
[114] Surah Yusuf, 12:33.

the authority on every subject—certainly as the expert in their respective field. To them, everything else is as insignificant as an ant, small and without value, unworthy of respect. Such people see nothing in front of them. They are preoccupied with indulging their egos. Arrogance is an effective guile that Satan uses to reach us, and so it is forbidden in Islam. Arrogance generates denial. Arrogant people are always in a state of rejection. They do not accept ideas, suggestions, opinions, common beliefs or common concerns from others, nor do they have respect for anyone. Arrogance is a state in which the belief God placed in the heart is rejected.

## THE OCEAN OF HUNGER

*When thy Lord drew forth from the Children of Adam -
from their loins - their descendants, and made them
testify concerning themselves, (saying): "Am I not your
Lord (who cherishes and sustains you)?"- They said:
"Yea! We do testify!" (This), lest ye should say on the
Day of Judgment: "Of this we were never mindful"*[115]

On the Day of Promises, when God assembled all the souls in His Presence, He asked, "Who am I and who are you?" The prophets and their companions replied, "You are our Lord and we are Your servants." With arrogance, even facing the power with which God had created them, everyone else answered, "You are who You are, and we are who we are." In reality, *"We are from God, and to God is our return."*[116]

God said concerning the creation of Prophet Adam ﷺ that He blew into him from His Power to give Adam ﷺ vitality.[117] Without that energy Adam ﷺ had been a helpless form of clay, unable to move. Thus arrogance belongs only to God, not to Adam ﷺ and his descendants. At that time all the seeds from which the human

---

[115] Suratu 'l-'Araf [The Heights], 7:172.
[116] Suratu 'l-Baqara [The Cow], 2:156.
[117] Suratu 's-Sajdah [The [Prostration], 32:9.

race would descend were placed in the back of Adam ﷺ. When the arrogant ones denied God's greatness by saying, "You are who You are, and we are who we are," God threw all their seeds into the Ocean of Hunger.

When you are hungry, you not only weaken, you lose your arrogance. If you are facing starvation, you eat anything you find. You quickly become humble. God humiliated them to the point that they said, "O Lord, we believe in You!" He then brought them out from the Ocean of Hunger, and again asked, "Who am I and who are you?" They knew then that they were nothing.

Prophets are innocent of any sin. The Prophet's Companions are also protected by God. However, normal people like us are sinners. We are weak. That is why God threw us into that Ocean of Hunger, so that when we came out, we believed. We said, "O Lord, you are our Lord and we are your servants." After we came into this world, we do good one day and wrong the next, circling between the two states, but in the end penitent from our sins, and so God has mercy on us. Those who were not believers continued to answer arrogantly, "You are who You are, and we are who we are."

This is the difference. It is difficult to find a person of faith with arrogance. Some may have it, but most do not. We fast to deny our stomachs, to keep us humble. We give charity to remember poverty and help the needy. Even in prayer, we bow down. So God has blessed us with ways to keep arrogance in check. May God protect and forgive us.

## 11. OSTENTATION (*AL-RIYA'*)

*Ah, woe unto worshippers who are heedless of their prayer; those who (want but) to be seen (of men), But refuse (to supply) (even) neighbourly needs.*[118]

Prophet Muhammad ﷺ said:

*God does not accept an action if there is any quantity of show in it.*[119]

The ones who show off are proud of what they do, and want everyone to know of their deeds. Good manners demand that we acknowledge the power of God in our achievements and our inability to achieve anything, save by God's mercy and grace. Showing off prevents us from recognizing God's role.

For example, a person is ill and goes to the doctor for treatment. That doctor prescribes medicine that cures the patient of his illness. We should not believe that the doctor cured the patient, which is a hidden form of associating others (*shirk*) with God. Rather, we must know that God cured that patient. If the doctor makes the mistake of thinking that he cured that patient, and he boasts about his efforts and the results achieved from his brilliant medical acumen, that doctor is trying to usurp God's position by casting himself as the healer. In reality, God is the Healer, and the doctor is an instrument of God's Will.

---

[118] Suratu 'l-Ma'un [The Orphan], 107:4-7.
[119] Imam Ghazali, *Ihya 'Ulum ud-Din* (*Revival of the Religious Sciences*).

Today, it has become commonplace for those who donate money to a cause or support a project to have their names inscribed on beautiful plaques for all to see, or to receive other awards and public recognition for their charity. But where did that money really come from? God gave that person money, and if God wanted otherwise, that person would have nothing. So, in reality, whatever a person donates is from God, not from them, as God is the Owner. So it is bad characteristic to take credit in such a situation. It is showing off. The one who shows off wants his or her name to be seen. If someone is doing something for the benefit of the community, yet celebrates his or her name, it is not accepted. Rather, it is showing off. May God forgive us from falling into this hidden form of *shirk*!

In the time of the Prophet ﷺ, a certain Companion liked to help people, but he also liked everyone to know that he did such good deeds. Concerning this, God revealed the last verse of the Chapter of the Cave:

> *Say: I am only a mortal like you. My Lord inspireth in*
> *me that your God is only One God. And whoever hopeth*
> *for the meeting with his Lord, let him do righteous work,*
> *and make none sharer of the worship due unto his*
> *Lord.*[120]

Imam Suyuti interpreted this verse in this manner:

God is saying, "If you are requesting to come to Me, to be in My Paradise on Judgment Day, you must do a good work, but that good work must not be accompanied by ostentation. Do not attribute that work to yourself, but to Me, as something which I granted to you personally."

The reason for revelation of this verse was that one of the Companions was in the habit of doing good things and afterwards saying to the Prophet ﷺ, "I did this! I did that!" He sought

---

[120] Suratu 'l-Kahf [The Cave], 18:111.

recognition. Then God revealed this verse.[121] By doing so, God is saying, "O Muhammad! Tell him that if he wants to do something good, let him do it, but make it purely for God, not for recognition for himself. It must be purely for Me."

When you do something, do it for God alone—not for anyone else. Surrender to God from the depths of your heart, without seeking anything in return. Often, when people receive something good, they mistakenly say, "We are getting our rewards from God." It means they are doing good deeds for a reward. The saints, who are higher in spiritual understanding, encourage us not to seek rewards. If God wants to reward you or not, leave it up to Him. You might win a greater reward than what you would ask for, so do not desire a small return! Seek His mercy and avoid the hidden form of idolatry, *shirk al-asghar*.[122] Believers do not associate anyone with God, including themselves when they do a good deed.

## THE CLEANSING OF DEATH

God wants to clean His servants. At death, God does not want to take the soul when it is in a state of hidden idolatry, *shirk al-khafi*, a state which He makes apparent in the body of the dying person. Because of this cleansing process, some people have difficulty breathing at the time of death. Others sweat profusely as God is cleaning their souls. Such people tried to live in the Way of God, but Satan played with them, but at the end, they repented. They see how merciful God is with them and feel shy, and so they sweat. God will remove the darkness of hidden idolatry when you are passing from this world. God said, *"We have honored the children of Adam."*[123] He honors us by cleansing us. He does not want believers to come to Him without being purified. He will clean us from the taint of ostentation, and from all the vices with

---

[121] Al-Hakim in *al-Mustadrak*.

[122] "the lesser idolatry," also known as *shirk al-khafee*, "the hidden idolatry."

[123] Suratu 'l-Isra [The Night Journey], 17:70.

which we are tainted, as long as we remember our contract on the Day of Promises, when we testified, "You are our Lord, and we are Your servants."

When God threw us into the Ocean of Hunger,[124] for 70,000 years, God gave us nothing but darkness. In that horrible separation, we hungered not only for food, but also for His love, His beauty, His mercy, His patience, His forgiveness and for all His beautiful Names and Attributes. May God keep us in His Presence and in Paradise with His prophets and messengers and the guiding masters of enlightenment.

---

[124] See the chapter on arrogance.

## 12. ATTACHMENT (*AL-HIRS*)

The Prophet ﷺ said:

> *The son of Adam ﷺ is heedless when two things grow within him: anxiety for wealth and anxiety to live long.*[125]

Attachment refers to the love of this world and all that is in it. People suffering from the disease of attachment desire long lives, and even if they live for a thousand years, they will never be satisfied, never saying, "Enough!" Prophet Muhammad ﷺ did not have attachment. The Angel of Death, Archangel 'Azrail, came to the Prophet ﷺ and said, "O Muhammad! Do you want to go to your Lord in the Divine Presence, or do you want to stay in this world? God is giving you the choice." The Prophet ﷺ was the only one in this universe to be given this choice, and he chose to go to God.

Sayyidina 'Ali ؏ said, "Do for the life of this world as if you will live forever, and do for the life of the next world as if you will die tomorrow."

Do not be greedy for this world; you will not live forever, and the next world is better, and in comparison to this, far more enduring.

> *Thou wilt indeed find them, of all people, most greedy of life, even more than the idolaters. Each one of them wishes he could be given a life of a thousand years, but the grant of such life will*

---

[125] Prophetic Tradition.

*not save him from due chastisement, for God sees well all that
they do.*[126]

Even if you live for a thousand years, you will not find genuine
benefit in this world. May God keep us from running after it.

## THE TWO MEANINGS OF ATTACHMENT

God said about the Prophet:

*Now hath come unto you an Messenger from amongst
yourselves: it grieves him that ye should perish: ardently anxious
is he over you* (harisun)*: to the Believers is he most kind and
merciful..*[127]

In this instance, the term *hirs* has taken a different, positive
meaning, referring to the Prophet's emotional attachment to his
Community. In the negative sense, *hirs* means to be attached to
this world and all its riches, to always want more to consume, to
never be satisfied with what you have. However, when *hirs* is for
God's sake, as the Prophet's ardent seeking of God's Mercy for
His servants, it is permitted. You can be attached to God and
hunger for more worship, blessing and mercy, but hunger for this
world is forbidden.

One must seek balance in life, which is achieved by following
the Divine Law. To seek fame and fortune and to have a good
time in this world are without foundation. Building for the
Hereafter increases our love for worshipping God and brings us
more honor, more divine favors and more dignity.

May God protect and forgive us.

---

[126] Suratu 'l-Baqara [The Cow], 2:96.
[127] Suratu 't-Tawbah [Repentance], 9:128.

## 13. SUPERIORITY (*AL-ʿAZHAMAH*)

*And certainly Pharaoh was lofty in the land; and most surely he was of the extravagant*[128]

Claiming greatness (*ʿadhama*) is a trait of Satan, who replied to God when He ordered him to bow before Adam ﷺ:

*I am better than Adam ﷺ! You created him from clay and me from fire, so why should I make prostration to him?*[129]

We must know our level as servants. We accepted submission (Islam), faith (*Iman*) and excellence (*Ihsan*), and we accepted the Prophet Muhammad ﷺ. Thus, we must follow our Prophet ﷺ, who never thought of himself as great in comparison with God. He was the most humble person.

Grandshaykh ʿAbd Allah al-Faʾiz ad-Daghestani ق tells a story which demonstrates this negative trait in human beings. A man was given a tank of water and his job was to distribute the water to thirsty travelers. People would come to him and he would pour the cold water in a cup and give it to them. One day he was overcome with conceit. He purchased a number of cups, and painted each one a different color. Whenever someone seeking refreshment came and reached for a cup of water, he would say, "No. Not that one, take the green cup." "No, not that cup, take the

---

[128] Surah Yunus [Jonah], 10:83.
[129] See Suratu 'l-Baqara [The Cow], 2:34 and Surah TaHa, 20:116.

red cup." By this means, his self was able to aggrandize to itself a power over people which was neither valid, necessary or useful.

To regard yourself as great is an indication that Satan is entering your veins. In the human body, blood travels through the veins to the heart, and in the heart there is a black clot *(mudgha).* The Prophet ﷺ said:

*Verily, there is a piece of flesh in the body. If it is good, the whole body is good. If it is bad, the whole body is bad.*[130]

That spot in the heart is where Satan enters and plays, turning humility to arrogance and making people strut like peacocks.

Alexander the Great conquered most of the world. Upon his death, he instructed his ministers that they must leave his hands outstretched from his tomb. "I want to show people that Alexander the Great left this world empty-handed," he said. Let this be an example to us all. You are going to die, and you will not take anything from this world with you except your good deeds. Regardless of how long you live in this world, one day you are going to leave it empty-handed. You are not the greatest. God is the Greatest, and that beautiful Divine Attribute is reserved exclusively for Him. To claim greatness is to claim something that is not ours, and so is akin to stealing. Greatness belongs to no one except God.

God described the Prophet ﷺ:

*Now hath come unto you a Messenger from amongst yourselves: it grieves him that ye should perish: ardently anxious is he over you: to the Believers is he most kind and merciful.*[131]

"Full of Pity" (*Ra'uf*) and "Merciful" (*Rahim*) are God's Names, which He shared with the Prophet. But God never shared the attribute of Greatness with anyone. We have no right to claim it and if we do, God will remove us from His Mercy. Be careful!

---

[130] Bukhari, Muslim, Ibn Majah, ad-Darimi, Ahmad.
[131] Suratu 't-Tawbah [Repentance], 9:28.

God told us to make prostration, which is the only way to kill any claim to greatness that lurks inside us. In the Holy Qur'an, there are fourteen points in the course of completing its recitation where we must prostrate. With them, God is reminding us, "Do not raise your head, for I am the Lord! Do not think you are great, for I am the Lord! Prostrate to Me." The saints took knowledge from the Prophet ﷺ regarding how to protect against the claim to greatness. Protection comes by the Prayer of Salvation and the prostration that follows it[132], or even by making one prostration after every prayer.

Satan approached the ancestor of all humankind and Prophet ﷺ, Adam ﵇, in Paradise and tempted him to eat from the forbidden tree, saying, *"It will give you everlasting life! It will make you great!"*[133] After he did so, Adam ﵇ knew that he had sinned. In repentance, he went into prostration for forty years. God then forgave him. On the other hand, Satan, before his fall from grace, was a devout servant of God, prostrated to Him on every handspan of God's creation, for he sought to be known as a devotee. But when God ordered him to prostrate before Adam ﵇, he refused. This even was not the end of his rebellion, for even after God had condemned him, he refused to seek forgiveness.

Grandshaykh 'Abd Allah ق related:

It is said that one time Satan came to a spiritual scholar, a saint, in a vision, and asked him this question, "God said, *'My Mercy encompasses everything'*[134] Am I included in that 'everything' or out of it?" That saint did not answer because that is in the realm of God's Will, so he left it alone saying neither "yes" nor "no."

Saints are always submitting to God's Will. They do not interfere in judging others, but focus only on their own selves. So

---

[132] See the chapter on Jealousy.

[133] Surah TaHa, 20:120.

[134] Suratu 'l-'Araf [The Heights], 7:156.

he looked at his own self, knowing that he is responsible only for his own actions, and the need to purify himself, and he left Satan's question unanswered. "Yes" would mean Satan is under God's Mercy, but because God has reviled Satan, he was afraid to tell him "yes." He was equally afraid to tell him "no" because God had said "everything" unconditionally. He was afraid to give either answer. So he gave none, putting down his ego's desire to give an answer and demonstrate superiority over the accursed Satan.

Grandshaykh 'Abd Allah ق told us:

It is further related that Satan asked this same question many hundred years later of another saint, who gave another answer. That answer boggles the mind but can never shake the heart. He said to him, "You fall within 'everything!' You are under the mercy of God!"

"Do you want forgiveness?" he asked. "Yes," Satan replied. "I recommend you do one thing," that saint said. "What is that?" Satan asked. "Go to Adam's grave and make prostration before it, repenting of your previous refusal, and it might be that God will forgive you, for that is in God's Hands."

"What?" Satan responded, "When he was alive I refused to prostrate before him. Now that he is dead and buried you want me to do that?" Thus Satan refused to lower himself, demonstrating his ultimate egoism, despite knowing full well he was in the wrong and that the result of his ongoing disobedience would be nothing but further disgrace. For Satan, the following verse of Qur'an is most appropriate:

> When it is said to him, "Fear God," he is led by
> arrogance to (more) crime.[135]

---

[135] Suratu 'l-Baqara [The Cow], 2:206.

Once the famous Sufi saint, Ibrahim ibn al-Adham ق was in a forest, for he used to wander about the earth, seeking the Divine Presence. It was snowing heavily and he found no shelter other than a hut built on top of some stairs. Under the stairs there was some space half covered by the snow, so he huddled there to take his rest and wait for dawn to appear. While he slept, three people came and climbed the stairs leading to that secluded room, bringing with them bottles of wine to drink. He wanted to sleep, but these people kept clanging the glasses together, toasting each other and carrying on. What did that saint do? He said only one word. He said, *"Alhamdulillah,"* meaning, as everyone understands it, "all praise is for God."

But to God it is completely different, for He knows intentions and He knows the hearts. As soon as Ibrahim ibn al-Adham ق said this, he heard a voice addressing him saying, "I shall throw you out of My Presence if you say it in this way another time!" At that moment, a drunk came out of the hut and seeing Ibrahim ibn al-Adham ق, scolded him, shouting "Why are you here?" God caused that drunk to go to do that, punishing Ibrahim ibn al-Adham ق for his saying "all praise is for God," in the way that he meant it.

Now let us explain: With what intention exactly had Ibrahim ibn al-Adham ق said, "all praise is for God?" He said it with the sense, "Thank God that my Lord did not make me like them, a drunkard, and that He has shown me His light and made me a good person." He praised God in that sense for which God was not pleased and admonished him. It is good to say, "all praise is for God," but not to say it in the sense, "I am better than them," with the intention of belittling others and aggrandizing yourself, thinking you are better than everyone. It is an aspect of God's Justice that He made some people one way and others another way. It was done in order for this world to move, and that is the wisdom behind it that human beings do not understand.

When Prophet Muhammad 🕌 was born, he immediately went into prostration. When Jesus Christ 🕌 was born and his mother took him to her people, he said, *"I am the servant of God."*[136] Such examples demonstrate how God wants us to relate to Him, with Him as the Greatest and us as His humble servants. May God protect us.

---

[136] Suratu 'l-Kahf [The Cave], 18:30.

## 14. HEEDLESSNESS AND LAZINESS
## (*AL-GHABAWAH WA 'L-KASALAH*)

*If laziness is slain so too is heedlessness.*[137]

Laziness and heedlessness are akin. Laziness is manifested in the inner self (*jawhar*), while heedlessness is located in the external self, the physical body (*jawareh*). Neglect becomes apparent when one behaves with the lowest level of intellectual energy, without care to apply oneself. If you ask someone with this spiritual illness even to answer the telephone, they will reply, "Ah! It's too much. I have no energy for that." If you suggest to them, "Let's go to the store and buy groceries for our dinner," they will make any excuse to avoid that. Such people are waiting for death. Such people waste their time and benefit neither themselves nor others.

God created twenty-four hours in each day. He said, *"O Muhammad! Say to them, 'Do!'"*[138]

There is a famous story of the great emperor, Harun ar-Rashid, whose generosity is renowned. He built a place where his subjects were provided food, shelter and clothing. Thus, they had no incentive to work. His brother Bahlul was a saint who observed that, because of this ease, the entire country was deteriorating.

---

[137] Arabic saying.
[138] Suratu 't-Tawbah [Repentance], 9:105.

Harun ar-Rashid consulted him about what needed to be done, and Bahlul assured his brother that he had a plan.

He started by going to the largest shelter and setting it on fire. The occupants ran out, all except for two who were unable even to run out of the building. Each was lying in his place with the fire about to surround them. One said, "Please move that way a little," to which the other replied, "No, *you* please move a little the other way." In this way, the pair proved that they really were unable to take care of themselves. A minister had them both removed and ordered that a large house be built for them, as they deserved to be attended to. As for the others, who were only pretending to be incapable, he ordered them to return to work.

Laziness is the internal manifestation of heedlessness. It afflicts the character and cannot be seen. The lazy one delays everything, as it holds no importance to him. He even delays prayer, good deeds and responsibility. Every goodness is escaping from his heart, even the love and fear of God. It is his nature to never help or intervene in any situation. If he sees that he has the solution to a problem and may in some way benefit others, he will still not render assistance. If the lazy one realizes society as whole, or even his own community, is facing a catastrophe and he knows how to prevent that catastrophe, he will not intervene. Rather he will let everyone suffer, because he likes everything and everyone to deteriorate along with himself.

May God protect us.

## 15. ANXIETY (*AL-HAMM*)

The Messenger of God ﷺ is reported to have said:
*Say often, "There is no strength nor power except God." Surely it is a treasure from Heaven, and in it is a healing for every malady, the least of which is anxiety.*

Another Prophetic Tradition relates that the Prophet ﷺ said:
*Whoever says, 'There is no God except God,' dispels from him ninety-nine tribulations, the least of which is anxiety.*

Worry develops from heedlessness. Anyone with this characteristic is heedless of the fact that God alone is the Provider (*ar-Razzaq*), and that He saves from every harm. Heedlessness of God, of the Prophet ﷺ, of Islam, of the Path and of the next world leads to excessive worry. People with this problem feel the burden of worry and do not know how to relieve it because they do not submit their lives and their hearts to God.

God says:

> *The Evil one threatens you with poverty and bids you to conduct unseemly. God promises you His forgiveness and bounties. And Allah cares for all and He knows all things.* [139]

Islam instructs us to submit to God in this life, to surrender our burdens and problems to God's care, to avoid carrying worry.

---

[139] Suratu 'l-Baqara [The Cow], 2:268.

That is why the saints never carry worry for this world; their concern is only for the Hereafter.

The Prophet ﷺ was worried about the position of his Community in the next world, not for what its members have in this world. When people asked him about how to conduct their trade, he gave them directions, and when that trade failed, they came protesting to the Prophet ﷺ. He ﷺ said, "I am teaching you to build your life for the next world, not for this world." Some heedless people have wrongfully interpreted this incident, claiming that the Prophet ﷺ made a mistake. We ask forgiveness of God for such a claim; the Prophet ﷺ does not make mistakes. He taught us not to ask him for this life, but to ask for the Hereafter. When you do not know, when you are heedless of God's plan that you must submit to, then you carry all the worries of this life.

## WORKING WITHOUT WORRY

Sayyidina Shaykh Sharafuddin ق, our great Grandshaykh, lived in a Turkish border town named Rashadiyya. In his time, the Ottoman era, the invading enemy armies were approaching the area. Villagers ran to him for advice, saying, "Their armies are two nights' distance from us! Should we leave this village?"

He answered, "No. Go and plant your crops."

They were astounded. "Plant our seeds?" they asked.

"Yes, you are safe," he said. "Do not worry about the enemy. Go and plant your seeds."

They followed his advice and planted their crops.

The next day the enemy continued to approach, and the villagers again came to Shaykh Sharafuddin ق, asking him what they should do. He said, "Leave the village."

Surprised, they implored, "Why? We planted the seeds, just like you told us!"

Shaykh Sharafuddin ق replied, "Do not be lazy! God gave you work in this life, so complete it."

The lesson here concerns how to discipline ourselves for the Hereafter. God made obligations for us in this life, such as taking care of our families, our health and our religious duties. Building for the next life is not just sitting with a rosary, praying and reading Qur'an, for the Prophet ﷺ said:

God The Exalted, loves a believer who engages in a lawful means of earning a living.[140]

If we fulfill our obligations to God, we will not have to worry about our future. God is taking care of that. We must try our best to work, to provide for our family, living within our means. Some earn more than others, according to what God has allocated, and we must be content with what He has given us. When you are content, you do not worry. When you do not worry, you will not be depressed.

---

[140] Tabarani, Bayhaqi.

## 16. DEPRESSION (*AL-GHAMM*)

*So We brought thee, (O Moses), back to thy mother, that
her eye might be cooled and she should not grieve.*[141]

A Prophetic Tradition states:

*Verily God, The Glorious and Majestic, by His wisdom and
exaltedness created ease and comfort in contentment and
certainty; and He created depression and fear in doubt and
discontent.*

Worrying is external. For the one in whom depression thrives,
this negative characteristic penetrates deep into the recesses of the
physical body, into the veins and heart. Such a person feels
depression in every part of the body and prefers to be alone rather
than see anyone.

A depressed person wishes that time would again fly, but, on
the contrary, minutes seem like hours, hours like days and days
like weeks. Usually, people who lack useful outlets for their
energies and feel unfulfilled are subject to these feelings. People
who suffer from depression tend to sleep all day and stay awake
at night, which allows them to avoid others. At night they engage
in frivolous activities that they find entertaining, such as watching
television, playing video games or some other pastime that gives
them pleasure.

May God forgive and protect us.

---

[141] Surah TaHa, 20:40.

## 17. THE EIGHT HUNDRED FORBIDDEN ACTS
### (*AL-MANHIYAT*)

*Those who avoid great sins and shameful deeds, only*
*(falling into) small faults,- verily thy Lord is ample in*
*forgiveness. He knows you well when He brings you out*
*of the earth, And when ye are hidden in your mothers'*
*wombs. Therefore justify not yourselves: He knows best*
*who it is that guards against evil.*[142]

There are 500 acts that the Prophet ﷺ ordered us to do (*ma'murat*) and 800 acts that the Prophet ﷺ forbade us (*manhiyat*) from doing.

The Prophet ﷺ said:

*To leave an atom's weight of God's prohibitions, is more lovely to*
*God than the worshipping of all sentient beings.*

To leave one forbidden act for the sake of God, is equivalent to performing all 500 of the ordered actions because to leave one forbidden act is extremely difficult for the ego.

Imam al-Qushayri noted that, of the 800 forbidden acts mentioned in the Holy Qur'an, 477 are grave ones (*min al-kaba'ir*). He mentioned further that if a person can eliminate the sixteen reprehensible characteristics that we have explained in the preceding sections, it becomes easy to avoid indulging in the the remaining forbidden acts. Thus the 800 forbidden acts are

---

142 Suratu 'n-Najm [The Star], 53:32.

considered one among the seventeen ruinous traits. We intend to describe these in further detail in another volume in the future.

As step three of the next section, in walking the Path to discipleship, the seeker must address this ruinous trait with the treatment of self-accounting, *muhasabah*. This method requires the seeker to keep a journal, and every day during his day-to-day activities note down every bad character trait that he observes in himself. These are traits that only he possesses, for no two individuals are the same.

When that journal if finally completed, it will detail a number of the 800 forbidden acts that individual possesses in his or her personality.

الخطوات العشُ

# THE TEN STEPS TO DISCIPLESHIP
## *AL-KHUTUWATU 'L-'ASHAR*

الهجرة و المراقبة

## MIGRATING AND MEDITATING
## (AL-HIJRAH WA 'L-MURAQABAH)

What is the real meaning of pilgrimage or migration? Can the real meaning be only moving from one city to another, or between countries or acquiring a new nationality? That is the physical meaning: leaving one place to go to another. Today the world has become a global village. You can be in many places, practically at the same time. Wherever you are—on the moon, or on a mountain—you can be in touch with every other part of the world by means of technology. You can run your business from the heights of the Himalayas if you have a computer and can connect to a satellite. This world has become so small that people are seeking to expand their territory. That is the reason they are trying to reach Mars, because they imagine that they can go there—even live there. Maybe that would be a real migration, because who goes there will never come back. Migration demands that you leave one place, but do not return. If you do, it is not a true migration.

The true spiritual migration, *hijrah*, is the one Prophet Muhammad ﷺ led his Companions on. It is his teachings. The Prophet's teachings embody the highest understanding of migration; he gave us the principles of migration in perfection. If we observe, experience and act on these principles, we will achieve the genuine migration that everyone is longing for. Not a migration from the Earth to Mars, or from the Earth to the Moon. Such a migration would still be within the boundaries of this world, for "this world" includes all that you can see of stars, planets and galaxies in space. What the Prophet ﷺ gave us is the migration of character, from corruption to purity, from ugliness to blessedness, from darkness to light. He taught us to understand moral values, and that by achieving perfection of character we gain God's satisfaction and happiness.

When you make the migration from bad desires and traits to good character and manners, when you achieve the highest level of moral virtue, you attain the power of spiritual ascension and self-realization. At that point, your ego stands at its limit, not transgressing the bounds of morality and manners. Wonders will be opened for you at that time. However, when you reach that level, do not pretend that such power or vision belongs to you; in reality, it is from God. Render everything back to its source: God's Divine Names and Attributes.

At that time, the real migration—the highest level of understanding—will open for you through your meditation, *muraqabah*. People long for that level, and try to practice meditation in every possible way to reach it. Some people imagine that they have achieved the highest level through their meditation, because they have reached whatever it was they were trying to reach. But beyond whatever they have achieved, there remain infinitely higher levels to reach.

People say, "We are meditating." But what are they meditating on? They say, "We are trying to connect with the highest universal energy, with the cosmos. We are trying to reach the Divine Presence..."

Meditation (*muraqabah*) is not something that you hold. It is like a prayer, a form of request. In truth, meditation has no structure, no form; it is universal. Everyone is thinking, and meditation is a thought. Indeed, it is no more than thought. Perhaps the thought comes to you to become an engineer. That is meditation. Studying medicine is meditation. Studying carpentry is meditation. Studying philosophy is meditation. Studying spirituality is also meditation. Meditation is not something that you acquire, but rather a means of obtaining something. When you reach what you were thinking of, your contemplation of it is no longer meditation, but something else since you have reached that which you were contemplating. Meditation is only a means of reaching, step by step. It is like a ladder. If the ladder is lost while you are climbing, you will fall down. However, once you reach the roof, the ladder is no longer needed, for you have reached your destination.

That is why the Prophet ﷺ said, *"An hour of thought (tafakkur) is better than seventy years of worship."* It is more effective than ordinary worship. It is faster in relation to such worship as a rocket is in relation to a car. Thus, the benefits of an hour accelerate to match the benefits of seventy years. [xii]

Do you see how much importance Prophet Muhammad ﷺ gave to meditation? Yet, it is only an aid to reach a certain level. When that level is reached, there is no more need for that kind of meditation. The meditative process is no longer properly called "meditation" once the object of meditation has been reached. People might object to the use of that word. Nevertheless, it is a reality and it is in the Holy Qur'an:

*Verily in that are Signs for those who reflect.*[143]

When you meditate and decide to leave bad characteristics and move toward good characteristics, then meditation becomes like a ladder you climb, ascending to higher and higher positions. As God says:

*And those who strive in Our (cause), We will certainly guide them to Our Ways: For verily God is with those who do right.*[144]

The Prophet ﷺ told the Companions, *"Now we are returning from the lesser jihad to the greater jihad."* The greater *jihad* is the fight

---

[143] Suratu 'r-Ra'd [Thunder], 13:3. This phrase is repeated verbatim in five other verses.
[144] Suratu 'l-'Ankabut [The Spider], 29:69.

against the ego. Those who struggle against the ego are the ones guided to Our Ways. This *jihad* is to oppose desire by means of what one does not like. To struggle with the ego means that whatever your ego asks, do otherwise.

Meditation in itself is not a struggle against the ego; therefore it is not the highest level. In fact, doing it makes you happy and might make your ego proud. You may say, "I am meditating; I am achieving something." When you think of and seek achievement and reward, what you are doing is not a pure form of meditation to God. You are still asking something in return for your actions. Saints never ask for anything in return for their worship. They understand that God created them and brought them to this world with His Will. Whatever they have to do, wherever they are taken, it is up to His Will. They are not asking for rewards or even for Paradise.

In contrast, some people are saying, "Give us the Divine Presence." That becomes like business or trade. It is as if they are saying, "Give us this, and we will give you that." At higher levels of spirituality, that is not accepted. At higher levels you must be like a dry leaf, blowing in the autumn breeze. The leaf does not say, "Why are you moving me right?" or "Why are you moving me left?" The leaf is like a sailing ship in the ocean, going where the wind takes it. Do not think that everything will be as you like. Sailing vessels on the ocean move according to the wind. That wind is not in your hands; it is in God's Hands.

If there is anything that you are seeking in meditation, it will never end. The steps on any ladder of meditation are endless. However, when you say, "O God, I am coming to You, asking nothing," then ascension takes less time. So say, "Whatever you want to do with Me, do, O my Lord. My religion is the religion of love; to love You is my religion. You sent Your messengers, Your prophets and You sent Prophet Muhammad ﷺ, and so I love You and I follow You."

Today they often speak of "unconditional love." Unconditional love is universal love. If you have that, then everyone is equal in your eyes, all human beings. God created them the same. You have ears, they have ears; you have eyes, they have eyes; you have a mouth and each one of them has a mouth. They are not different. They are the same.

God gave three sets of points to all of us. One set has seven focal points that we must recognize and observe. Another set has four such important points. Another set has nine. Four, seven and nine: these numbers are linked to the fundamental arithmetic and essential composition of your body. By studying them, you will learn that arithmetic and you will understand that composition. If we keep the group of four, the group of seven and the group of nine points clean, then we achieve something.

The first group, comprised of four points, is named the "Secret," "Secret of the Secret," "Hidden," and "Most Hidden." These four levels are found in the mystery of the heart.

Four other points have been given to us in accordance with the Prophet's ﷺ saying:

*My servant continues to approach Me through voluntary worship until I love him. And when I love him I will be the ears with which he hears, I will be the eyes with which he sees... "*

Thus, the ears and the eyes are four points. The saying continues:

*...I will be the tongue with which he speaks, I will be the hand with which he acts, and I will be the foot with which he walks.*[145]

Here are three additional points, completing the group of seven. These seven points are very important for us. The order in which the aforementioned actions are listed is significant. The last step in this is walking, whereas you begin with ears, eyes, tongue and hand. When you establish your seeing and hearing, when you are able to hear and see what people do not hear and see, then you will receive guidance. Then you can speak. Then you will be given

[145] Bukhari.

a power of the hand, to change whatever you like in this world, for the Prophet ﷺ said:

*Whoever sees something wrong, should try to change it with his hands...*[146]

One action you can take with your hand is to sign something. To sign a paper has significance in this world. When you sign the Divine Agreement then too will all things change; then you will be walking on the Straight Path.

The nine points are represented by the Enneagram. We must activate these points in order to reach a higher level of meditation.

God ordered us as Muslims to make ablution first. In ablution, the first thing we do is take water into our hands and wash them. We wash and then pass our fingers between each other. If you look at your hands, you will see the number 18 written in Arabic on the right hand and the number 81 written in Arabic on the left. Together, these numbers add up to 99.

Arabic Numerals: Left 81; Right 18

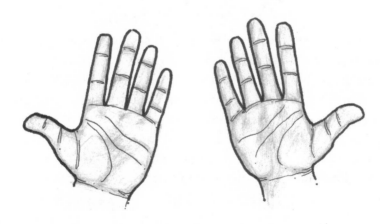

---

[146] Narrated with a variety of similar phrasings in Muslim, Ahmad, Tirmidhi, Abu Dawud and Ibn Majah. The remainder of the hadith is "and if he is unable, then by his tongue, and if he is unable to do that, then through his heart, and that is the weakest of faith."

There are 99 Beautiful Names and Attributes for God. By washing and rubbing your hands you begin to activate the energy of the hands, entering that Divine Code. In numerology, 18 and 81 each resolve to nine. Nine and nine added together is 18, and that again reduces numerologically to nine. Beyond nine, the zero is introduced. That point of nothingness is at the center of the Enneagram, where real migration leads.

## ABOUT THE *QIBLAH*

People reach the East, West, North and South, yet wherever they go their focus is one—the *Qiblah*. God said that when you want to pray, direct your face towards God's Holy House, the Ka'ba:

> *We see thee (O Muhammad) turning of thy face for*
> *guidance to the heavens: now Shall We turn thee to a*
> *Qiblah that shall please thee. Turn then Thy face in the*
> *direction of the Sacred Mosque [Ka'ba]: Wherever ye are,*
> *turn your faces in that direction. The people of the Book*
> *know well that that is the truth from their Lord. Nor is*
> *God unmindful of what they do.*[147]

Wherever you are, direct your face towards the mosque of the Ka'ba in Makkah. Because of the presence of the Ka'ba, the place around it is holy. That place is called the *Haram*, meaning "prohibited;" it is a place where sins are prohibited, a sanctuary. Even bad intentions in its Holy Precincts are written against you. It is called a mosque, but God made it more than that. In reality, it is a place where sins cannot be accepted. That is why its Arabic name is *Masjid al-Haram*, the "Prohibited Mosque.[148]

> *Glory to (God) Who did take His servant for a Journey*
> *by night from the Sacred Mosque to the farthest Mosque,*
> *whose precincts We did bless, in order that We might*

---

[147] Suratu 'l-Baqara [The Cow], 2:144.
[148] Also translated as the "Sacred Mosque."

*show him some of Our Signs: for He is the One Who*
*heareth and seeth (all things).*[149]

Wherever this place is mentioned, it is always *Masjid al-Haram*. The name *Masjid al-Haram* means that no one may act on bad desires there—no one may even have bad thoughts there. Only good desires and good thoughts are accepted, not the characteristics of animals. Animals act without any limits on their behavior. So "*Masjid al-Haram*" means the mosque where degrading behavior is unacceptable. The best symbol of ignorance is the donkey. When people have this characteristic, we will describe them as exhibiting "donkeyness." Today, people carry this characteristic. Their ignorance leads them to bestial behavior, and they perform all kinds of unacceptable actions.

Each person has the aim and hope to reach a holy place, and for Muslims that place is the *Masjid al-Haram*. The Muslim's focus is to reach a perfected level of character, to learn from it and to be enlightened from it. God knows the heart. According to your sincerity and achievement, God connects you to your aim.

*Those who struggle for Us, We will guide them in the*
*right ways, the ways that are suitable to them.*[150]

There are levels of achievement. We must progress beyond our state of ignorance, learning and educating ourselves by keeping the company of an enlightened person.

God says:

*O ye who believe! Fear God and be with those who are*
*true (in word and deed).*[151]

The polished heart of the sincere and true believer (*sadiq*) is the receptacle for God's heavenly lights and divine blessings to manifest. Such a person is to us like the sun. When the sun rises, the whole world shines from that source of energy that makes all

---

[149] Suratu 'l-Isra [The Night Journey], 17:1.
[150] Suratu 'l-'Ankabut [The Spider], 29:69.
[151] Suratu 't-Tawbah [Repentance], 9:119.

things visible. It was dark and then it shines. According to your personality and according to how much you free yourself from "donkeyness," to that extent God grants you higher levels.

The focus of everyone is, and must be, the holy place. If we achieve something but still carry our "donkeyness," we begin to imagine that we know something. If we know something, we must act on it and follow it according to our understanding.

## FOLLOWING TRUE LEADERS

It is related that the Prophet said:

*Leaders will be appointed over you who reflect your behavior, characteristics and personality.*[152]

There are leaders that we mistakenly follow out of ignorance. Such leaders also mistakenly think, through their own ignorance, that they are real leaders. They "guide," but in reality we do not improve through them. To the extent that you free yourself from "donkeyness," you will be connected with a higher level of leaders that will take you quickly to enlightenment.

"Donkeyness" increases arrogance in us. You cannot accept any advice if you suffer from "donkeyness." Arrogance makes people refuse to accept anything except themselves.

A shaykh, or someone who leads or guides, must be connected through a lineage of shaykhs to the Prophet. Not everyone who says, "I am a shaykh," becomes a genuine shaykh. You may have permission to conduct *dhikr*, but anyone can perform *dhikr*. The ability to guide and give advice is not open to just anyone. That is not in the hands of ordinary people.

There are six powers of the heart opened at the first level of discipleship. If these powers are missing, a person has not become a genuine disciple (*murid*). Outside the Circle of Disciples is the Circle of Lovers, those who love the Prophet ﷺ and the saints.

---

[152] Ibn Najjar in his *Tarikh*.

Those in this circle do whatever they can, but they have not yet polished themselves to reach the level of discipleship.

God gave these six powers to all of humanity, because everyone is born in Islam.[153] These levels are within you, but you need to purify yourself in order to reach them. You cannot reach them until you reach the level of being a disciple and your guides open them.

The six powers are:

- ❖ The Reality of Attraction
- ❖ The Reality of Heavenly Blessings[154]
- ❖ The Reality of Focus and Healing[155]
- ❖ The Reality of Intercession
- ❖ The Reality of Moving in Space[156]
- ❖ The Reality of Guidance

At the first level of discipleship, you will see all of these six powers. Thus, it is only necessary to ask those claiming to be shaykhs to list the six levels of the heart that are opened to the disciple on the Way of the Knowers to determine whether they really are what they claim to be. If they do not, how can they be a guide? They may be storytellers. That is fine, for at least it gives blessings. But such a person must neither deceive himself nor the people attending him into thinking he is something that he is not.

Once people had Bayazid al-Bistami ق arrested and sent to the king. It was determined that he was to be executed.[xiii] So, escorted by soldiers on horses, he was led through the desert to the king.

---

[153] "Human beings are born in innocence." Bukhari.

[154] This refers to the power of disciples to attract heavenly blessings upon themselves.

[155] This refers to the power of disciples to use the eyes of their heart concentrate Divine Energy like a laser beam, direct it at a person and cure them.

[156] This refers to the power of disciples to appear in one place while their body remains in another place.

In a dream, the king saw Prophet Muhammad ﷺ, who warned him of the approach of one of his saints through the desert and urged him to go and see him. The king persisted in his sleep, and saw the same dream again. Again he slept and saw the same dream. At last, he awoke, called his ministers and army, and set out by horse. Bayazid ق was seven days away.

The king dismounted when he reached Bayazid al-Bistami ق and walked to him. Lifting that saint's chains, he put Bayazid ق upon his horse and led him back to the palace on foot. It took him several days to walk back. He took Bayazid ق into the palace, showered him, rubbed his back and hid him in a place where people would not be able to find him. Everyone was afraid of the king's punishment.

After seven or eight days, hundreds of Bayazid's followers came to the doors of that palace. The king wondered who had leaked the information concerning his hiding of Bayazid ق, and asked his followers how they had come to know. They said, "We followed the footprints of light that led to this palace." They were able to trace his steps based on the light that came from the path that he had traveled.

Sainthood is not a joke, nor is the power of Guidance. It is not for just anyone to claim the power to guide. It is very important to connect to a genuine shaykh. If you connect with a real shaykh, you can fly. But if you connect with a shaykh who, though pious, has not reached true sainthood, you will only be walking. That is because the saintly shaykhs are connected to the Divine Presence.

When you have these six powers and you open your mouth to speak, there are people with receivers who listen to your broadcast from the main station. At that time, you are the source, no longer transmitting what was said by others.

Today, they have live broadcasts and recorded broadcasts. The recorded ones are excerpted from live broadcasts. The resulting recording may be outdated and old-fashioned, like old tape recorders; half-way through, the tape may break, and then you have to splice it back together. The Shaykh of Blessing (*Shaykh al-*

*Baraka*) is like that. However, with the shaykh that is connected to the Divine Presence, angels, spiritual beings and saints are all listening to him, receiving information when he speaks.

As soon as you say "*Allah*," anyone with a receiver can receive. It is a wave. It does not die, it continues. That is why it is always being written. If you program your computer to say "*Allah ... Allah ...*," it will keep doing so until Judgment Day without stopping. That wavelength mentioning the Name "*Allah*" is moving. You can receive that wavelength if you have a receiver and extract the sound from it. That is the big difference between a true Shaykh of Guidance (*irshad*) and a Shaykh of Blessing.

For one on the real path to sainthood, the first level to be achieved is wakefulness. This is the level of readiness and awareness—awareness of God's Divine Presence, of His watching you. One who has reached that level is always aware of what is going to happen. You must be aware of everything around you that takes you away from God.

Beware, because at any moment your ego may bring you down. Do not let the "donkeyness" of your ego overcome you. Do not allow your ego to order you to do this or that. You have to submit to God. If you listen to and obey your ego's whims and desires, running towards what it wants and fleeing what it hates, then watch out. A moment of heedlessness might be enough to destroy you completely. That is why you need a guide.

Take the analogy of a lawyer. To protect his clients, a lawyer may tell him not to do things that, though they may seem innocuous, are in fact illegal. He, or she, may advise against things that are technically legal, but have the appearance of impropriety or illegality. He may advise against legal actions that could lead to unlawful behavior. The lawyer wants to eliminate any chance that his client will be sued or face criminal prosecution. Thus, a lawyer becomes an instrument for informing his client about these pitfalls and preventing them from transgressing into unlawful behavior. Lawyers remind you. They know that one mistake is enough. You might make a thousand mistakes without being seen, but if one of those mistakes is discovered, then you will be in trouble.

Similarly, if you drive your car with a police officer sitting beside you in the passenger seat, you will not drive too fast, but dutifully observe all the rules and regulations of the road. Knowing that he would stop you, you refrain.

The tricks of Satan and the ego can make you fall immediately. Not having a spiritual "lawyer," a guide, is like being heedless of the laws that the police around you enforce. A real shaykh is such a spiritual advocate. Using the powers of telepathy (see Reality of Focusing) that God bestowed upon him, he is able to warn you. He is able to communicate through your heart, even when he is far away, helping you remain aware and avoid heedlessness. Thus, you become conscious of anything that might lead you into error. In this way, enlightenment begins to take over your heart.

Perhaps *all* our actions are heedless, and perhaps they might all pass by, unseen or forgiven. But one heedless act that is not forgiven can destroy us completely. The guide keeps us from that one act, just as the lawyer protects us from behavior that transgresses the law. We are under the shaykh's microscope, and he is checking us.

This is the first of the ten different levels on the way of gnostics that you must achieve. Reach these ten levels, and only then will you open the six powers that are in your heart.

We must focus our attention on the same point that all Muslims focus on, the *Masjid al-Haram*. That is the place where no sin can be committed. The heart of the believer must be treated the same way, for God said, "My heavens and My Earth cannot contain Me, but the heart of My believer can contain Me." By following this Way, the heart becomes like the *Masjid al-Haram*, a place where sins are prohibited. It becomes a place dedicated to God.

*The Prophet Muhammad ﷺ said: "There is not one among you but a comrade from among the jinn is assigned to him." They (the Companions present) said: "Even you, O Messenger of*

*God?" He* 🕮 *said: "Even me, but God granted me victory over him and he became Muslim, so he only enjoins me to do that which is good."*[157]

We cannot throw our devils out, but we have to keep struggling against them. We are weak servants. O our Lord, if You do not support us, we fail; with Your support, we succeed.

---

[157] Muslim.

## THE FOCUS OF THE HEART

The heart is a place that has to be clean, for it is narrated that God said, *"The heart of the believer is the house of the Lord."*[xiv] Revelations come to the Prophet ﷺ; inspirations come to the hearts of regular people. Since the focus is the heart, you have to keep it clean.

When you have a house you clean it every day. You vacuum and mop it in order that it will appear clean in your eyes and in the eyes of your guests. If you keep your house clean, then what about what God has entrusted to you to keep clean. God is saying to us, "I am giving you My Home, where all inspirations come, through which all blessings come to you. How are you going to receive My inspirations? Are you going to receive them in a finely polished heart, or are in a tarnished, cloudy heart?" It is very important to purify our hearts from the corruption of this world. It is also important to remove the pollution of those whose negative energy affects us in our lives and destroys the respect that God put in our hearts for Him. Today, unfortunately, people are respecting Satan more than they are respecting the Merciful Lord.

A shaykh guides his followers to the Way of God. Everyone's focus in this world should be directed towards the *Masjid al-Haram*, which is the reality of the heart. Again, the Prophet ﷺ said, *"The heart of the believer is the House of the Lord."* God said that the Ka'ba is His House. For your heart to become like a Ka'ba, everything there must be clean. You cannot go to the Ka'ba and do something wrong. It is prohibited. One sin committed there might be equal to 100,000 sins elsewhere, just as one prayer there is valued as much as 100,000 prayers said elsewhere.

There are cars today that drive using batteries. Others use diesel, while still others use gasoline. Each type has a different ability. If you want to go sixty miles an hour, you can use a car that runs on batteries, but they cannot go faster than that. If you want to go faster, you may use a diesel car. If you want to go faster still, you use gasoline. If you want to move even faster, there is jet fuel.

The guide gives you a daily *dhikr* to recite in order to clean your heart. The daily *dhikr* is designed to make you reach different levels of the heart. In meditation, people say, "O my Lord, we are coming to You." They connect their hearts to their shaykh's heart, from his heart, to the Prophet 🕊, and from the Prophet 🕊 to God. That is the way and it is acceptable, but you cannot come to that practice with a dirty heart. You cannot connect to the Divine Presence and contemplate God's Beautiful Names and Attributes with a dirty heart, just as you cannot sit in a dirty house or use a dirty prayer rug to pray.

So many people make mistakes in their meditation. They make *dhikr*—"*Allah, Allah*" or "*La ilaha ill-Allah*,"[158] —and focus on that. That is good, but before you do that you must meditate and reflect on the negativity in yourself, on your sins, on your own bad character. At night, take a notebook and pen, and write down what you did during the day, starting with the moment you woke up. When you wake up, it is *sunnah* to renew your Testimony of Faith, *shahada*, because it is a new day. Did you do that? If not, account for it as one mistake. After that, you must perform ablution. Did you do that? If not, record it as another mistake. Proceed like this, step-by-step, and record all of your mistakes. This record will become a journal of your sins and mistakes: "I spoke harshly with my wife… I went to work and sold an item to a customer for $10 when the fair price was $5… I stole… I cheated… I lied… I was walking on the street, saw something forbidden, and did not look down…"

---

[158] There is no god but God.

In Islam, we know that there are 500 good actions to be done and 800 forbidden actions that the Prophet ﷺ ordered us to avoid. Before you begin to meditate on God through *dhikr*, you have to meditate on how to throw the dirt—your donkey-like characteristics and ignorance—from your heart. That is why the Prophet ﷺ said, *"To contemplate for one hour is better than seventy years of worship."*

Audit yourself. If the government tax office comes and says, "We want to audit you," what would you do? You would be worried that they might find a mistake, even though you tried your best not to make any mistakes. You might tremble. If you tremble before the tax auditor, how do you think you will be before God, when He calls you to be audited?

> *Then shall anyone who has done an atom's weight of good, see it!*[159]

Do you not believe in the Day that is coming? For saints, that Day is every day. Their disciples must audit themselves. If you audit yourself, it is as if you prayed for seventy years.

One time Grandshaykh 'Abd Allah ق said, "It is very easy to pray two cycles of prayer or to fast one day, but it is very difficult to leave one forbidden action." For example, you look at something forbidden and keep looking, because your ego does not let you stop. All of us are dipped and dumped in forbidden actions. Anger is one of the worst characteristics. The Prophet Muhammad ﷺ said, *"Anger is unbelief."* Who does not have anger? You cannot claim that you do not have it; the truth is that you blow up at everyone.

It is most important to look at our negative characteristics. The shaykh, when he looks at you, knows what kind of negativity you are harboring. Spiritual guides list ten steps that you have to take when you embark on your journey seeking knowledge.

---

[159] Suratu 'l-Zalzala [The Earthquake], 99:7.

الاستقامة

## 1. STANDING UP FOR TRUTH
### (*AL-ISTIQAMAH*)

*Say: "I do admonish you on one point: that ye do stand*
*up before God,- (It may be) in pairs, or (it may be)*
*singly,- and reflect (within yourselves): your*
*Companion is not possessed: he is no less than a warner*
*to you, in face of a terrible Penalty."*[160]

To stand up for God means to stand up for Truth against falsehood. Who is standing up for Truth against falsehood today? Before looking at others to judge them, stand for Truth against the wrong within. Fight against the devil in yourself. Stand for God against Satan, because Satan is always there, gossiping in your heart. To stand for The Merciful means to keep your eyes open and to be aware of all that is within yourself. This leads to self-realization.

Look at yourself in the mirror of your teacher and guide, and see how many bad characteristics you can count. By becoming aware of these negative characteristics, you become aware that God is observing you and you know that you must come before His Presence. You have to stand up for Him. To do so, you have to eliminate your destructive character traits.

---

[160] Surah Saba [Sheba], 34:46.

## VIGILANCE (*AL-MURAQABAH*) المراقبة

Awareness counters heedlessness. If someone is heedless, he is careless of consequences, unaware of the results of his actions. You should be aware constantly, keeping your defenses up. What is the spiritual weapon of a believer? Ablution.

The Prophet Muhammad ﷺ said:

*Ablution is the weapon of the believer.*[161]

Ablution purifies you and opens all your cells to receive innumerable blessings and to manifest the beautiful Divine Attributes.

There are animals that cannot see, but that have antennae. There are blind people who cannot see, but who carry a cane. Antennae and canes are used to gatherer information. For such people, these are sensors, gathering information about what is around them. As they interact with the world through their sensors, people and animals become aware of any dangers lurking nearby.

When you wake up on a dark night and have to walk in the dark, you may do so with your hands extended so that you can feel your way. You use your senses. Spiritual awareness means that your whole body is aware of Satan and his traps. Without this awareness, you may be lost in heedlessness. One moment of heedlessness is enough to destroy you. You do not know when God's Anger will come on you, therefore you must be aware and avoid actions that are prohibited.

Al-Junayd ق said:

My teacher in the way of vigilance, *muraqabah*, is the cat: One day, I was passing in the street, I saw a cat sitting and watching the hole of a mouse, so absorbed in its hole that not one of its hairs was moving. I was bemused by its concentration and watchfulness, and I was called in my innermost: "O you with the weak

---

[161] Arabic: *Al-wudu silaah ul-mu'min.*

determination! Do not let me be in your purpose less than the mouse, and you, do not be in the seeking less than the cat." So I awoke, adhered to the path of vigilance, and achieved the results that I did.

When through vigilance, you try to distance yourself from heedlessness, your heart will stand up for God. You will become aware of everything about you and will thereby begin to eliminate Satan's interference. Eliminate heedlessness, and your heart will begin to be clean and polished. The tarnish will be removed and light will come. When you are standing for God, He will bless you and shower you with His light, and thus your heart will become enlightened.

The Prophet ﷺ said:

*The faith of a person will not be upon firmness and obedience to God (istiqamah), until his heart is standing forth for God. And his heart will not be standing forth for God, until his tongue is standing forth for God.*[162]

## SELF-AWARENESS (*AL-YAQAZAH*) اليقظة

Wakefulness, *al-yaqazah*, is the first level, the beginning of the journey of the gnostic. In the Sufi Path, *tariqat*, there are three ranks: the beginner, *mubtadi'*, the prepared, *musta'id*, and the disciple, *murid*. When you reach that level of awareness, the level of standing up for God, you are traveling between the level of preparedness, *musta'id*, and the level of the disciple, *murid*. There are ten steps you have to climb in order to reach the level of disciple. This is the first.

Meditate on the negativity in your heart. Now, as you meditate, you are like someone playing with a toy. When you raise yourself up through the ten levels, the six powers will be opened to you. Then you will no longer be playing with a toy vehicle, like a child, but will have a real vehicle to drive. You will

[162] Ahmad.

begin to visualize and hear genuine inspirations. However, you must first eliminate negativity from your heart, and stop oppression of your soul. God says:

> O ye who believe! stand out firmly for justice, as witnesses to God, even as against yourselves, or your parents, or your kin, and whether it be (against) rich or poor: for God can best protect both. Follow not the lusts lest ye swerve, and if ye distort (justice) or decline to do justice, verily God is well- acquainted with all that ye do.[163]

When you are no longer an oppressor, you will be dressed in the attribute of justice. One who has that attribute is the opposite of an oppressor. Justice is to stand up for God against Satan, worldly attractions, lust and the conspiring, egocentric self, and to walk the Straight Path, deviating neither to the right nor to the left.

May God forgive us.

---

[163] Suratu 'n-Nisa [Women], 4:135.

## 2. REPENTING THROUGH THE PROPHET
### (*AT-TAWBAH*)

*And those who turn not in repentance, such are evil-doers.* [164]

We are still beginners, trying to find our way on a long journey. It is a long journey because it is full of obstacles. Something full of difficulties always seems long. Time passes quickly if you entertain yourself, but someone busy with work sees the time leading up to his vacation as unending. The journey of self-realization is long, but at its end you will reach true happiness, feeling the pleasure of God's remembrance, *dhikrullah*. Know that, until you reach your goal, you will face many obstacles.

When you want to repent, God will remove you from the list of oppressors.

*And those who turn not in repentance, such are evil-doers.* [165]

Do not despair of God's mercy. God will forgive; God is Most Great. God says in the Holy Qur'an:

*Say: "O my Servants who have transgressed against their souls! Despair not of the Mercy of God, for God forgives all sins. He is Oft-Forgiving, Most Merciful."* [166]

---

[164] Suratu 'l-Hujurat [The Private Apartments], 49:11
[165] Suratu 'l-Hujurat, 49:11.
[166] Suratu 'l-Zumar [The Groups], 39:53.

And in another verse:

> .... *If they had only, when they were unjust to themselves, come unto thee (O Muhammad) and asked God's forgiveness, and the Messenger had asked forgiveness for them, they would have found God indeed Oft-returning, Most Merciful.*[167]

And in a third verse:

> *We sent thee not (O Muhammad) but as a Mercy for all creatures.*[168]

Do not lose hope, because Muhammad ﷺ is with you, and he will intercede for you. Do not lose hope for God's Mercy; because of the Prophet Muhammad ﷺ, God will forgive all sins. When you put these verses together, you see that the Prophet Muhammad ﷺ *is* the mercy that God sends, and He is telling those who have oppressed their own souls not to lose hope. Ask for intercession and God's forgiveness at the door of the Prophet ﷺ. In order to approach that door, you must audit yourself and make an accounting. Then you can ask forgiveness.

How do you ask for forgiveness? You say, "I did this wrong, I seek forgiveness, (*astaghfirullah*)." The Prophet ﷺ is obliged to ask forgiveness for those who ask for it. Once they have the Prophet's ﷺ official approval, the repentant ones will find God Forgiving and Merciful. This is the second level, to repent through the Prophet ﷺ, after identifying one's bad characteristics in the first level.

When you realize that you are a sinner with problems, you also realize that you need an intercessor—someone who is more sincere—to take you by the hand. The most sincere, the best intercessor, is the Prophet Muhammad ﷺ. However, you cannot go directly to the Prophet ﷺ either. You also need someone who is

---

[167] Suratu 'n-Nisa [Women], 4:64.
[168] Suratu 'l-Anbiya [The Prophets], 21:107.

an inheritor of the Prophet ﷺ, who knows the obstacles you face and who will take you by the hand.

> *If they had only, when they were unjust to themselves,*
> *come unto thee (O Muhammad) and asked God's*
> *forgiveness, and the Messenger had asked forgiveness for*
> *them ...*[169]

There are different sorts of instruments to cut vegetation. There are lawnmowers, some better than others, and there are tractors. However, if you go into the jungle in Africa or Southeast Asia, you cannot enter with such machines. You need a bulldozer. You might even need dynamite to clear the land. If your guide is like a lawnmower, he may clear a small area before you. If he is more powerful, he may clear further. If he is like a bulldozer, he will be able to clear a wide space, and if he is like dynamite, then he can open a road for you to reach your destination, even through many tremendous and stubborn obstacles.

You need an inheritor who has followed the way and traversed the entire journey, who can look at you and guide you through your heart. Your responsibility is to audit yourself.

---

[169] Suratu 'n-Nisa [Women], 4:64.

## 3. AUDITING (*AL-MUHASABAH*)

*O ye who believe! Fear God, and let every soul look to
what (provision) he has sent forth for the morrow. Yea,
fear God, for God is well acquainted with (all) that ye
do.*[170]

This verse shows that the soul, not the body, has to prepare
provision for the next life. That is why you must begin keeping
track of all your negative issues. This can only be done by taking
up the weapon of the pen against your enemy, the ego.

How do you audit yourself?

'Umar ibn al-Khattab ☙, the second caliph of the Prophet ☙,
said:

*Judge yourselves before you are judged; and weigh your actions
in the balance before they are weighed; When you are brought to
account tomorrow, it will be much easier for you if you have
already brought yourself to account today...*[171]

This step involves auditing yourself by keeping a journal of
your deeds, much as the Recording Angels are doing. Once you
begin noting down the wrong actions that you do throughout the
day, you will end up with a journal full of negative issues. Those
who do not take account cannot repent. How do they know that
they have done something wrong? When you audit yourself, you

---

[170] Suratu 'l-Hashr [The Gathering], 59:18.
[171] Ahmad and Abu Nu'aym.

will see your wrongdoing. Anyone who fails to stop his wrong action is an oppressor, a tyrant. Of course everyone is doing wrong, but only those who fail to repent are oppressors.

Do not just say at the end of the day, "O God, I committed many mistakes today, forgive me." Rather you must write them down and repent for each mistake in turn. Then turn the page for the next day. The next day you make mistakes, and you write them down. Then you correlate them to see if they are new ones or the same. In this way, you enter a period of self-discovery, identifying all kinds of bad manners and harmful traits that you never actually realized that you had. These bad characteristics thereby become known to you, and so you must repent from them. God will remove the ones who do so from the "list of oppressors."

Continue to record your bad characteristics and bad manners every day. In three to six months, you will have found 200 to 300 bad characteristics. When you eliminate these, you will be ready to receive the manifestations that come to someone titled "disciple."

After you decide to repent, and you begin to audit yourself and observe your base desires, your real journey begins. In your audit, you will discover what you have done wrong. Then you must repent from your bad actions and vices. Write down every forbidden act you have committed and decide for yourself whether you will do that act again, or move forward and improve.

*Once a Bedouin came in the midst of the Friday prayer sermon and asked the Prophet ﷺ when Judgment Day would occur. At first the Prophet ﷺ did not answer him, but continued delivering the sermon. The Bedouin asked a second time, and the Prophet ﷺ still did not answer. Then the Bedouin asked again—showing real zeal, passion and concern—so Archangel Gabriel ﷺ came and said to the Prophet ﷺ, "Answer him. He is sincere."*

*The Prophet ﷺ said, "It is a long way to the Day of Judgment. Why are you asking? What kind of provision have you put aside for that day?"*

The meaning of this statement is that the way to that Day is full of difficulties and problems. Every step along the way, you are stepping with your ego, confidently trusting in your personal devil, following his direction wherever he tells you to go and continuing to obey your evil inclinations. This is the situation we are in. So the statement "It is a long way" is, in itself, an admonition to prepare. What are you expecting? What are we preparing? We need bulldozers and dynamite to clear our way to that Day if we wish it to be a happy one for us.

*And take a provision (With you) for the journey, but the best of provisions is right conduct.*[172]

The Bedouin was sincere, pure, a lover. He was someone who understood wisdom. *Thus, he answered, "Love for you, O Messenger of God."*

This means, "I do not have anything. What am I going to find? How am I going to solve my problem? How am I going to make my journey without your love? Your love is my beacon, my flashlight, my spotlight, my sun, my moon and all the stars in my universe, guiding me as the North Star guides everyone."

*And by the stars (men) guide themselves.*[173]

When you are moving in life or in spirituality, you always have to make sure that you are moving higher, improving. Just as north is the highest reference, so the Prophet ﷺ is north. He is the central reference point for all spiritual travel, the guide for everything, the North Star of spiritual navigation.[174]

*O ye who believe! Fear God, and let every soul look to what (provision) he has sent forth for the morrow. Yea,*

---

[172] Suratu 'l-Baqara [The Cow], 2:197.
[173] Suratu 'n-Nahl [The Bee], 16:16.
[174] The North Star is called *qutb* (pole) in Arabic; this word is also applied to the highest spiritual authority in any particular domain.

*fear God, for God is well acquainted with (all) that ye
do.*[175]

At the time of your meeting Him, you will fear God. If you
have done something wrong and have not provided for your
future, then you will have nothing. If you do not fear Him, you
will not have provided anything for your afterlife.

The Prophet ﷺ was pleased with seven groups of people
whom God will shade on Judgment Day from its awful heat and
terrifying fear. One is a girl or boy raised in obedience to God.[176] If
you fulfilled the covenant that you made with God on the Day of
Promises and did what God asked you to do in your lifetime, you
will be saved. Otherwise, you are a loser. That is why you have to
repent. You must provide for your soul by repenting from the sins
that your body has done. Ask repentance for the sake of piety, of
keeping sincerity with God. When you have sincerity and piety,
God will teach you.

*... If ye do (harm to them) lo! it is a sin in you. Keep
piety and be aware of God . God will teach you, and God
is Knower of all things.*[177]

When you have love for the Prophet Muhammad ﷺ, and are
showing your love by moving with your guide through the jungle
of the dark aspect of the self, then God will tell you, "That is
enough sincerity for Me. I know you are weak. I know Satan is
after you, just as he was after Adam—but you need that love.
Before you come to My love, you have to come to the love of the
Prophet ﷺ."

As the Bedouin said, he had prepared only love for the
Messenger of God.

---

[175] Suratu 'l-Hashr [The Gathering], 59:18. C.f. also, *"(Then) shall each soul know
what it hath sent forward and (what it hath) kept back."* Suratu 'l-Infitar [The
Cleaving], 82:5.
[176] Bukhari, an-Nisa'i, *Muwatta* Malik, Tirmidhi.
[177] Suratu 'l-Baqara [The Cow], 2:282.

*The Prophet ﷺ said to the Bedouin, "That is enough, because you will be with the one whom you love."[178]*

Thus the Bedouin's love to the Prophet ﷺ was sufficient to bring to be with the Prophet ﷺ on Judgment Day. The Bedouin did not even enter the mosque after talking to the Prophet ﷺ. Instead he just walked away, because he was so happy, so overwhelmed that the Prophet ﷺ had spoken to him. That event was so immense for him. He felt as a person would feel when addressed by a king, or a president—very happy that someone in such a high position recognized him. However, for that Bedouin, his feeling was beyond that, since the Best of Creation told him that his love was enough. It overwhelmed him, and he did not know what to do. When the Prophet ﷺ said, "It is enough," he left. He was an innocent person, with no impurities in his heart. It was clean.

That event was also immense for everyone present. The narrator of this Prophetic Tradition, Anas bin Malik ﷺ, said that the Companions never rejoiced as much as they did when they heard this Prophetic Tradition.

Love for the Prophet ﷺ is a sign of sincerity. There are many people who do not love God. They are falling into so many difficulties, and they do not know why. But there are some people who love God; and God said, *"Be pious and sincere and God will teach you."[179]* God also said, *"Above every knower is one more knowing."[180]* That means He will keep raising you through levels of knowledge, giving you knowledge upon knowledge.

When the Lord teaches you through inspiration to your heart, you learn what you have never heard; that which it is impossible to learn through books. Traditional scholars, masters like Imam Ghazzali ق, Ibn 'Arabi ق, Shah Naqshband ق, Ahmad al-Faruqi ق

---

[178] Bukhari and Muslim.
[179] Suratu 'l-Baqarah [The Cow], 2:282.
[180] Surah Yusuf [Joseph], 12:76.

and Jan-i-Janan[xv] ق received knowledge from God through their hearts. They were among the giants of Islamic scholarship, like the Companions. So, too, were the four Imams of the Divine Law able to write and explain jurisprudence because God inspired their hearts. Such knowledge filters down from higher levels.

The engine that endlessly produces this knowledge is piety and sincerity: *"Be pious and sincere and God will teach you."*[181] In this manner, you can learn more and more. If you fail to learn through sincerity and piety, you will be lost, unable to cross the jungle of your negativity. Sometimes in the jungle, the trees grow very close together and space is so cramped that you cannot even move—the way is very difficult.

People take their beads and make remembrance of God, *dhikr*. However, the correct way is not to do *dhikr* first. The correct way is to eliminate your mistakes first. To recite God's Name *"Allah, Allah"* 5,000 times may take fifteen minutes. To recite the holy words, *"There is no diety except God—La ilaha ill Allah"* 1,000 times may take seven minutes. Such practices are simple, but what is truly difficult is to prevent yourself from looking at what is forbidden. Grandshaykh 'Abd Allah ق said that if you see something wrong once, it is not written against you; however, the second look is forbidden. If you see something wrong, look away and say, "O my Lord, that is prohibited." This is far better than doing 500 obligations. Leaving one forbidden thing is more valuable to God because it is stepping on your ego and leaving a sin for His sake. It is very difficult to leave something that you desire, that the ego wants, yet this is what we need to do.

Do not leave *dhikr*; but also work every day to eliminate your sins. For each one that you have counted, you have to say, *"Astaghfirullah*—I repent, and I am not going to repeat that sin." That is the level of auditing. That is the level of reaching the point where every soul must check what it has provided for its future.

---

[181] Suratu 'l-Baqarah [The Cow], 2:282.

That is the way to reach the next level on the way to becoming a disciple.

Shaykhs do not block the whispers of your devils. They want you to block those whispers yourself. When you reach the level of a true disciple, then they will block the whispers. Until you reach that point, they want you to develop yourself. When you become a disciple, they protect and maintain the light that you have. A true disciple is like a receiver for the shaykhs; they see through his eyes, they hear with his ears, they act with his hands.

When you are in the presence of the shaykh, countless dark insinuations come to the heart. When you are in his presence, he is causing that gossip to "upload." All those bad whispers are being uplifted from the heart and purged.[xvi]

How does the shaykh hear all his students? He does so through a digital connection, not analog. Even without initiation, if it is written for you to be in the shaykh's group, he will test you—although you will be unaware of it. Some people might not even take initiation physically, but they were assigned on the Day of Promises to be in his group. Some people see Shaykh Nazim ق in a dream before ever having met him in this life, and then they go to meet him in the physical dimension.

## 4. TURNING HUMBLY TO YOUR LORD IN SURRENDER (*AL-INABAH*)

*Turn ye to our Lord (in repentance) and bow to His (Will), before the penalty comes on you: after that ye shall not be helped.*[182]

The seeker who has stepped forth on the way to find truth and reality needs a guide to open that way, to lead him to the presence of the Prophet ﷺ. The second step is to become aware of your shortcomings, and then you must repent and account for your actions. The fourth step is to turn humbly in surrender to your Lord—the essence of Islam. However the faith of Islam, consists of three levels, as described by the Prophet ﷺ in the famous Tradition of the Archangel Gabriel, where 'Umar ؓ related:

> While we were sitting with God's Messenger ﷺ one day, all of a sudden a man came up to us. He wore exceedingly white clothes. His hair was jet-black. There was no sign of travel on his person. None of us knew him. He went to sit near the Prophet ﷺ, leaning his knees against the knees of the Prophet ﷺ and placing his hands on his thighs.
>
> He said, "O Muhammad! tell me about Islam (the stage of Submission)." God's Messenger ﷺ said, "Islam is to bear witness that there is no god but God, and that Muhammad ﷺ is the Messenger of God; to perform the prayer; to pay the poor-tax;

---

[182] Suratu 'z-Zumar [The Groups], 39:54.

*to fast during Ramadan; and to make the pilgrimage to [God's] House if you are able to go there." The man said, "You have spoken the truth."*

*We wondered at him; how could he be asking the Prophet ﷺ and confirming him at the same time?*

*Then he said, "Tell me about Iman (the stage of Belief)." The Prophet ﷺ said, "Iman is to believe in God, His angels, His books, His messengers, and the Last Day; and to believe in Destiny, both its good and its evil."*

*The man said, "You have spoken the truth. Now tell me about Ihsan (the stage of Excellence of character)." The Prophet ﷺ replied, "Excellence is to worship God as if you see Him, for if you do not see Him, He certainly sees you."*

*...Then he left and time passed. Later he [the Prophet] said to me, "O 'Umar, do you know who that was asking questions?" I said, "God and His Messenger know best." He said, "He was none other than Gabriel. He came to you to teach you your religion."*[xvii]

This Prophetic Tradition illustrates that the religion consists of three major stages, the first being Islam, Surrender, the second being *Iman*, Belief, and the third *Ihsan*, Excellence of character. In the ten steps to discipleship we are describing, the first three steps are necessary to bring the aspirant from a state of disobedience and rebellion into a state of surrender to God's Will; the stage of Islam.

This surrender is what your Lord wants from you. This step, of turning back to God (*al-inaba*), in itself becomes a turning point in your life. This turning point starts with entering into Islam fully without mixing it with sins. God says:

> *O ye who believe! Enter into Islam whole-heartedly; and follow not the footsteps of the evil one; for he is to you an avowed enemy.*[183]

---

[183] Suratu 'l-Baqara [The Cow], 2:208.

Though you already went through the process of eliminating the seventeen ruinous traits, in the process of stepping forth on the Path to the Divine Presence, as you purify yourself further, you will unearth further negative traits from which you must turn away. This is a repetitive process, for the purer you become, the more apparent are your faults, and your consciousness of them is enhanced. Thus you must return again and again to take stock in an ongoing process of refinement.

The following represent the chief character defects that you must shed as you turn back to God. They represent the principal negative qualities that you must watch for and eliminate through the audit you make of yourself every day. Some of these are from the seventeen ruinous traits; others, while not as severe, nonetheless need to be eliminated at this stage.

The Prophet ﷺ said:

*God the Exalted revealed to Musa ibn 'Imran (Moses) in the Torah that the sources of all mistakes are three: arrogance, envy and greed.*"[184]

## ELEVEN DEFECTS THAT MUST BE ELIMINATED

Eight of these eleven defects are from the seventeen ruinous traits and they are arrogance, envy, greed, anger, rancor, stinginess, ostentation and love of fame and praise. Three additional traits are: praising the rich, despising the poor, and cheating.

## 1. ARROGANCE (*AL-KIBR*)     الكِبر

Sufyan ath-Thawri said:

*Every act of disobedience committed due to passion, its forgiveness is hoped for. Every act of disobedience committed due to arrogance, its forgiveness is not hoped for, because the root of*

---

[184] Ibn Hajar al-Asqalani.

*Satan's disobedience was arrogance, whereas the root of Adam's lapse was passion.*[185]

## 2. ENVY (*AL-HASAD*)

Another bad characteristic is envy, for instance envy of a rich person, or even a poor person, or a wise person or a healthy person. It is even possible for you to be envious of yourself.

## 3. GREED (*AT-TAMA'*)

Wahb ibn Munabbih al-Yamani ﷺ said:

*It is written in the Torah: He who is greedy is in fact poor, even if he owns the whole world.*[186]

## 4. ANGER (*AL-GHADAB*)

*The Prophet is reported to have said, "Anger corrupts belief."*

## 5. RANCOR (*AL-GHILL*)

*And We shall remove from their hearts any lurking sense of injury; beneath them will be rivers flowing; and they shall say: "Praise be to God, who has guided us to this (felicity)."*[187]

One bad characteristic that God does not like is to have rancor in your heart against your brother, against your community or against all humanity. Rancor has many aspects. You might manifest it by saying to yourself, "I am fed up with so-and-so." That rancor might be like an ember burning in your heart against your wife, your sister, your brother or your children. Or it might be against the community, the nation, the Companions or even against the Prophet ﷺ. You might even say, "What is the

---

[185] Ibn Hajar al-Asqalani.

[186] Ibn Hajar al-Asqalani.

[187] Suratu 'l-'Araf [The Heights], 7:43.

difference between me and the Prophet ﷺ? I am educated and he was not."

## 6. LOVE OF FAME AND PRAISE (*TALABU 'L-'ULUW*)

طلب العلو

Ibn Mas'ud ؓ said:

*How many are duped by the praise heaped on them.*[188]

Love of praise is another bad characteristic. You do not need people to give you importance; you need God to give you importance.

The Prophet ﷺ said:

*My companions are like the stars.*[189]

Despite this, not one Companion put a description of himself in front of his name. It has become a widespread spiritual disease that everyone needs to have some honorific added to the front of his name. Speakers will not speak at conferences unless you put all kinds of titles in front of their names. Before a conference, a speaker might give you a biography thirty pages long, with his entire life story, listing every paper he wrote, and every conference at which he has spoken.

Say, "I am no one. I am seeking truth and truth cannot be reached without leaving my ego behind and becoming nothing."

People like to be praised. If you do not praise them, they get upset; so you have to keep praising everyone. While introducing speakers, people praise what they have done through their lives. What is the value in this? Are they praising the person to make the ego more arrogant?

---

[188] Citied by Ibn Hajar al-Asqalani, *Preparing for the Day of Judgment.*
[189] 'Abd ibn Humayd's, al-Daraqutni's *Fada'il as-Sahaba*, al-Bayhaqi in *al-Madkhal*, al-Bazzar, (*da'eef*).

## 7. OSTENTATION (*AR-RIYA'*)     الرياء

*And be not like those who started from their homes*
*insolently and to be seen of men, and to hinder (men)*
*from the path of God. For God compasseth round about*
*all that they do.*[190]

## 8. STINGINESS (*AL-BUKHL*)     البخل

Abu Bakr as-Siddiq ❀ said:

*The miser will not escape one of seven things: either he will die*
*and the one who will inherit his wealth will spend it in that*
*which God has forbidden; or God will empower a tyrant over him*
*who will take his wealth from him after humiliating him; or He*
*will inflame in him a desire that will cause him to lose his*
*wealth; or he will have the idea of constructing a building in an*
*unsuitable piece of land and will thus waste his wealth; or one of*
*the calamities of this worldly life such as drowning, burning,*
*theft, or similar things will befall; or he will be afflicted with a*
*permanent illness and will spend his wealth seeking a cure; or he*
*will bury his wealth in a place which he forgets and thus will*
*never find it again.*[191]

## 9. PRAISING THE RICH (*MADHU 'L-AGHNIYA'*)     مدح الاغنياء

The Prophet ❀ said:

*The one who humbles himself in front of the rich man because of*
*his wealth will have lost two-thirds of his religion.*[192]

Praising the rich in order to collect their favors is another bad
characteristic. Forget their favors and the scraps that fall from
their tables, and seek the Favor of the One who is Source of riches,
al-Ghani.

---

[190] Suratu 'l-Anfal [The Spoils of War], 8:47.
[191] Ibn Hajar al-Asqalani.
[192] Ibn Hajar al-Asqalani.

## 10. DESPISING THE POOR (*IHTIQARU 'L-FUQARA'*)

Despising the poor is another negative quality. Some people ignore the poor and seek the company of the rich in order to collect the drops of wealth that fall from them. It is better to keep in mind the supplication of our Prophet:

*O God, let me live poor and let me die poor and raise me to life (in the Hereafter) among the poor.*[193]

## 11. CHEATING (*AL-GHISHSH*)

Cheating is another negative characteristic: not deceiving, but cheating. You can cheat by selling something for more than it is actually worth.

For example, when you put it on the scale, you claim that it is heavier than it is—perhaps saying two pounds instead of one. That is cheating in business, which also affects your spirituality. You can also cheat in spirituality by cheating against yourself, the Prophet ﷺ, the Companions, the four Imams or against God. You are cheating them when you sin. Looking at something forbidden, *haram*, is an example of this sort of cheating.

### THE TURNING POINT: THE EIGHT STAGES OF TRUTH

When you begin to be aware of yourself, repent of your sins and audit yourself you are at a major crossroads; you have made a 180 degree turn in your life: Crossing over from disobedience to submission and obedience. Having now entered wholeheartedly into Islam, one now begins the journey through Faith (*Iman*).

The Prophet ﷺ said:

*Faith is to believe in God, His angels, His books, His messengers, and the Last Day; and to believe in Destiny, both its good and its evil.*

---

[193] Tirmidhi.

This spiritual junction between Islam and Faith leads to the Eight Stages of Truth. In this process of turning which is the fourth step of discipleship, you must progress through eight sub-stages. Keep these eight stages in your mind as you turn.

## 1. FAITH IN TRUTH
## (AL-IMANU BI 'L-HAQQ)

الإيمان بالحق

Truth is the source of happiness. You have to believe in Truth. God is the Truth; that is one of His Attributes, Haqq—thus the connection of this stage to the first pillar of faith. The attribute of Truth will dress you at that turning point, so you must have faith that your turning point has arrived and that Truth will be your guide to reality.

> And say: "Truth has (now) arrived, and Falsehood
> perished for Falsehood is (by its nature) bound to
> perish."[194]

You have progressed through three steps in your self-realization journey, and so have come to faith in Truth. Truth will guide you to peacefulness, to the "Self at Peace."[195]

Faith in Truth will lead you to several important abilities that will further advance your spiritual progress.

## 2. TRUE DECISION(QARARU 'L-HAQQ)

قرار الحق

Faith in Truth will give you a true vision of everything. Until you reach this point, you are in a tunnel, walking behind that bulldozer that is breaking through the jungle.

Now you have to make the right decisions. You must become so simple and so peaceful that you do not harm any creature. Not one creature must receive any harm from you. You must distance your ego from harming anything, even an ant or a mosquito. Each

---

[194] Suratu 'l-Isra [The Night Journey], 17:81.
[195] A technical term in Sufism, an-Nafsu 'l-mutma'inna (the Self at Peace) is distinct from an-Nafsu 'l-ammara (the Self that compels to evil) and Nafsu 'l-lawwama (the Blaming Self).

creature is praising God; if you kill it, you stop its praising. You make the right decisions when you are peaceful, in submission to God's Will. You must keep your harm from everyone whether from speech, eyes, hand or any other organ. In the first three levels, this is not emphasized, but at the fourth level it becomes the key in life.

Hasan son of 'Ali ibn Abi Talib ♣ said:

*May God grant mercy to the servant who hesitates at the point of evaluation, and then if he sees the action is for God, he carries it out, and if he sees it is for something other than God, he avoids completing it.*

People who achieve this level of attention are considered saints by others. Many people may think, "Such a person is a saint, one of the Five Poles, a Changed One, a great shaykh." But they have not yet reached any of these high stations. Indeed, such a person has not even reached the level of disciple. He or she has only reached the level of making the right decision.

This stage is related to the second pillar of faith: belief in God's angels, for they are carriers of inspiration from the angelic realm to human hearts.

## 3. THE WORD OF TRUTH (*KALAMU 'L-HAQQ*)

كلام الحق

When the seeker learns to make the right decisions and knows not to inflict harm by any means, then he learns to speak the word of Truth. What he says is from the Ocean of Truth and Reality. He cannot speak what is not the truth—no lying, cheating, conspiracy, hating or backbiting. At that time, only the right words are spoken.

The word of Truth appears when you distance yourself from lying, backbiting and other harsh words. All the words you speak will be good, and so you establish that what you say is the truth.

The Word of Truth is related to the third pillar of faith: God's Holy Books.

## 4. TRUE BEHAVIOR
## (*SULUKU 'L-HAQQ*)

With faith in Truth, decisions from Truth and the word of Truth, comes true behavior. That means eliminating from your behavior and your character the sins of stealing and killing.

True behavior is related to the fourth pillar of faith: belief in God's prophets, for they were the exemplars of behavior based on the Word of Truth, which they brought in the revelation they received from God. The highest exemplar among all the prophets was Prophet Muhammad 🕊, about whom his wife Ayesha 🌸 said:

*His character was the Qur'an.*[196]

As an example, the sin of "stealing" includes so many actions that people do every day. If you look at someone you are not allowed to look at, that is stealing, which is why they say "stealing a glance." If you go to a place with a sign on the door that says, "Visits by appointment only," but then go to the window and look inside without an appointment, that is stealing. Looking at something you do not own is stealing. If I have a book on a table, and you come and open it, that is stealing. You have to ask my permission first. In a library it is acceptable, but with a private collection it is not. This is true behavior.

By "killing," we mean cutting someone down with harsh words—that is not accepted.

*And be moderate in thy pace, and lower thy voice; for the*
*harshest of sounds without doubt is the braying of the*
*donkey*[197]

Anything you do that you regret later, you must stop doing. That is the behavior of Truth.

---

[196] Ahmad.
[197] Surah Luqman, 31:19.

## 5. TRUE ACTION (*'AMALU 'L-HAQQ*)  عمل الحق

When your faith is true, and your decisions, your words, and your behavior are true, then you will establish the action of Truth. True action means leaving bad actions.

This stage is preparation for the reality of Judgment Day, in which the truth of all your actions will be shown, to yourself and to all others, standing before God.

People asked someone with very good manners, "How did you learn goodness?" He replied, "I learned from someone who is not good. Whatever he would do, I would avoid."

Many kinds of good action come under true action and may be written in your journal in the ongoing process of auditing yourself, *muhasabah*.

## 6. THE STRUGGLE OF TRUTH (*JUHDU 'L-HAQQ*)  جهد الحق

After you reach the action of Truth, the sixth stage is the struggle of Truth. When you want to do everything good, it is an inner struggle. Not everyone can do what is good all the time. The struggle of Truth is to look always for a good purpose, for something to benefit others, and to run away from anything evil. That is related to Destiny and what is foreordained of good.

## 7. THE MEDITATION OF TRUTH (*TA'AMULU 'L-HAQQ*)  تأمل الحق

When you have developed the first six stages of the fourth level, you come to the meditation of Truth. Before you were not able to focus; now you can focus with tranquility. You are peaceful; nothing disturbs you.

At this stage, you must surrender to events and accept any moment that comes in your life, and this relates to the seventh pillar of faith, Destiny and what it brings of difficulty. Good and bad must be the same to you. If anyone harms you or praises you, it will be the same to you. You will not show any unhappiness when someone harms you, and you will not show any happiness when someone praises you.

'Umar ibn 'Abd al-'Aziz ق said:

I have nothing that gives me any joy, except what God decrees to happen.[198]

When this state settles in your heart, at that time, when you contemplate, you will begin to concentrate and focus.

## 8. TRUE CONCENTRATION (*TARKIZU 'L-HAQQ*)

تركيز الحق

Look carefully and you begin to know where you are looking. When you are contemplating, you are unable to look, since your focus is through your heart. Where are you going to put your feet, and where are you going to touch your hand?

True concentration cannot be reached except by completing the seven stages listed above. At that time, you will reach the highest perfection in your behavior, the state of *Ihsan*, the "Self at Peace." That will be your key to fulfilling God's words:

> *Turn ye to our Lord (in repentance) and bow to His (Will), before the Penalty comes on you; after that ye shall not be helped.*[199]

Once you turn to your Lord, you will not lose. You will have no problems in your life. There will be a penalty only if you fail to turn. Those who succeed in turning will be included among those granted safety and protection from anything that might hurt them in the future.

By reaching this point, you will be establishing good. Every action you do will have life—a form and energy. When your good action has a structure, its life will come from the secret of sincerity that God puts into that action. Then you will be able to achieve what seekers are trying to achieve.

---

[198] Ibn Hajar al-Asqalani.
[199] Suratu 'z-Zumar [The Groups], 39:54.

There is a saying in Arabic that the disciple must accompany a shaykh that is on the right way. The guide must have completed the eight stages listed above; he must have completed the journey and rid himself of his bad desires. To such a shaykh, you submit and give your hand. You must always obey him. Do not hesitate. Hesitation brings doubts. It is a trick of the ego. It is also said that whoever does not have a shaykh, his shaykh is Satan, who is always at the ready to misguide.

Abu ʿAli ath-Thaqafi ق, one of the most significant figures in Islam, said:

A man who gathers all the knowledge of the world, and studies it and meets with all kinds of people to the point that he becomes a walking encyclopedia, will never reach the level of manhood, except under the discipline of a true shaykh and by undergoing seclusion under his supervision.

The "humble turning" is fourth in the ten levels you must pass in order to become a disciple, and within this one level are the eight different stages that we have listed related to Truth. You must watch and record these in your journal, thinking forward and back, and know your own level in reference to them. Then you will know where you stand.

## 5. CONTEMPLATING DEEPLY (*AT-TAFAKKUR*)

*We sent them) with Clear Signs and Books of dark*
*prophecies; and We have sent down unto thee (also) the*
*Message; that thou mayest explain clearly to men what*
*is sent for them, and that they may give thought.*[200]

This way, our journey, is the Way of Saints. They focused their best efforts throughout their lives in order to reach a higher level of enlightenment and spiritual understanding, to reach the highest degree of unseen reality through the power of gnosis. That power is higher than any power you can imagine. Gnostics have spent their lives trying their best on this way, and they laid the foundations for us to follow and to learn what they inherited from the Prophet ﷺ along their spiritual journey. As they laid the foundation for us, we must try our best to imitate them, because they are real and we are plastic. Plastic fruit looks real, but it is not real. We hope that God the Powerful will change us as He changed them, from plastic to real.

The foundations of being a disciple are ten, and we have listed four of these levels already: the first level is a general sense of self-awareness, the second is repentance in light of this new self-awareness, the third is a personal inventory of daily actions, the fourth is a 180-degree turn in the journey of the seeker. The

---

[200] Suratu 'n-Nahl [The Bee], 16:44.

turning point itself is considered a level, which marks the end of the first two sections of the journey: Islam and *Iman*.

The fifth step in our path is described in the Holy Qur'an:

> *He it is Who showeth you his Signs, and sendeth down*
> *sustenance for you from the sky; but only those receive*
> *admonition who turn (to God)...*[201]

Here, God is saying, "We have sent down to them the remembrance of the Holy Qur'an, after providing for them their lives and all that they want; and we have sent down to you, O Muhammad, the Holy Qur'an, in order that they may give thought."

The fifth level is deep contemplation. God sent the Holy Qur'an in order for us to contemplate it, not as something to play with, or to read without comprehension. He wants us to reflect on every word. Whoever gives it due consideration will understand the meaning of the Prophet's ﷺ saying, *"An hour's reflection is rewarded more than seventy years of worship."* If you follow God's Holy Commandment to spend time in contemplation, He will give you provision for the next world. God gave you material provision in this world and said, "My order and prohibition against sins are provision for your soul."

In the Holy Qur'an, God has stated everything. If you do not reflect on it, you will be lost.

> *Men who celebrate the praises of God, standing, sitting*
> *and lying down on their sides, and contemplate the*
> *(wonders of) creation in the heavens and the earth, (With*
> *the thought): "Our Lord! Not for naught Hast Thou*
> *created (all) this! Glory to Thee! Give us salvation from*
> *the penalty of the Fire."*[202]

In every moment, God is asking us to remember Him. That does not mean only to remember Him with our minds, but also to bring

---

[201] Suratu 'l-Ghafir [The Forgiver], 40:13.
[202] Surat Ali 'Imran [Family of 'Imran], 3:191.

the name of God to our tongue and to keep it moist with reciting His Holy Names and Attributes, *dhikr*. *"Standing, sitting and lying down"* is one phrase, to which is added *"and contemplate."* We have to reflect on the creation of the heavens and earth because He wants us to constantly realize His greatness.

To truly know there is a God, we must reflect on His Existence. The Prophet Abraham ﷺ at first considered a star as his lord, until it disappeared. Then he saw the moon and wanted to worship it, until it also disappeared. Finally, he turned to the sun, before realizing it too would disappear. God wants us to reflect in order to believe. He does not want us to believe only because we inherited religion from our parents. He wants us to have contentment, to believe because we consciously decided, "Yes, God is a reality."

That is the fifth level, and the beginning of the second phase of the journey. Seekers of the way, after completing the first phase, ask what they have to do to prepare for the second. The answer is to give the Holy Qur'an thought, consideration and earnest contemplation.

التَّذَكُّر

## 6. REMEMBERING YOUR SUBCONSCIOUS
### (*AT-TADHAKKUR*)

*He it is Who showeth you his Signs, and sendeth down
sustenance for you from the sky: but only those receive
admonition who turn (to God).*[203]

The sixth level is remembrance. Remembrance is higher than
contemplation. Remembrance will bring you into the Divine
Presence. In remembrance, you understand why water descends
from high on the mountain and why fire gives heat and power.
You begin to tap into your subconscious memory, which can
recall even the smallest atom that God brought into existence, and
the purpose that it serves in creation.

At this stage, the shaykh will order you into seclusion. This is
necessary for disciples on the sixth level. During the seclusion,
God will open to you the wisdom in every plant and animal,
including its benefit for you specifically and for mankind in
general. That is why everything comes to very high-ranking saints
during their extended seclusions. This we learned from
Grandshaykh 'Abd Allah al-Fa'izi ad-Daghestani ق and Mawlana
Shaykh Nazim ق, from their long seclusions over periods of years
and years, during which they learned everything that is of benefit
to every human being. These saints learn what kinds of plants can
be used for particular sicknesses and how to know, just by looking

---

[203] Suratu 'l-Ghafir [The Forgiver], 40:13.

at people, what kinds of problems and spiritual illnesses they are carrying. Then they can prescribe the exact medication to relieve them of the difficulties they face.

During this level of remembrance, you learn the reality of affairs. You will gain true enlightenment concerning the events in the world around you and in the larger universe. When you reach this level, good tidings come to you, for you have overridden your self. Good tidings come to you, because you have found the Truth. The Truth, noble and beautiful, will save you from devils and evil.

You have to trust the reality that is opened to you at that time; you cannot step back. Some seekers of the way, when they begin to understand reality at the sixth level, experience its bitterness. When you try to cut a rose bloom from its branch, you may be pricked by its thorns. It hurts, which is why people do not like to cut them. However, once you have cut the flower, you will experience its sweetness and smell. When the seeker is reaching the station of true discipleship, and so entering sainthood, he will soon feel a decrease in this bitterness.

Some people retreat because they cannot tolerate the difficulty and bitterness of the path, but you must not run away. You must endure it long enough to reach the best you can, for this life and the hereafter. The one who endures suffering and persists in the discipline will be able to enter and penetrate the shore of Divine Reality. He or she will become a knower in the Way of the Divine Presence. To achieve this rank you must have strong faith. If you remain diligent and constant while experiencing the sour taste of attainment, it will be the best of what can happen to you.

## 7. HOLDING FAST (*AL-'ITISAM*)

*And hold fast, all together, by the rope which God
(stretches out for you), and be not divided among
yourselves; and remember with gratitude God's favor on
you, for ye were enemies and He joined your hearts in
love, so that by His Grace, ye became brethren; and ye
were on the brink of the pit of Fire, and He saved you
from it. Thus doth God make His Signs clear to you:
That ye may be guided.*[204]


*And strive in His cause as ye ought to strive (with
sincerity and under discipline). He has chosen you, and
has imposed no difficulties on you in religion; it is the
religion of your father Abraham. It is He Who has
named you Muslims, both before and in this
(Revelation); that the Messenger may be a witness for
you, and ye be witnesses for mankind! So establish
regular Prayer, give regular Charity, and hold fast to
God. He is your Protector - the Best to protect and the
Best to help!*[205]

Once you have attained the sixth level of remembrance, which
ends with the first unveiling of sainthood, you will never want to

---

[204] Suratu 'n-Nisa [Women], 3:103.
[205] Suratu 'l-Hajj [Pilgrimage], 22:78.

step back again. You will be among those God describes in the preceding verses.

The Knowledge of Certainty is the Reality of Hearing. The Eye of Certainty is the Reality of Seeing. The Truth of Certainty is the Certainty of Reality.[206]

## THE PRESENCE OF SAINTS

The first of these realities relates to love for the shaykh, love for the Prophet ﷺ and love for God.[207] The Knowledge of Certainty, or the Reality of Hearing, includes hearing about your shaykh, hearing about the Prophet ﷺ and hearing much about God. When you keep hearing more and more, the shaykhs take you to a higher level where you establish full love of the shaykh, love of the Prophet ﷺ and love of God. At that level of love, it is as if you are in their presence; you will feel them.

When you love someone very much, he or she is always on your mind. When a man loves his wife very much, he cannot envision anything but her. No matter where he turns his face, he sees the image of his wife. What about when that love and adoration is directed with innocence and sincerity towards the Prophet ﷺ and the shaykh? Once you have achieved that presence and love, you will move towards the Presence of God through the Presence of the Prophet ﷺ and the Presence of the shaykh[208]. All of these relate to the Reality of spiritual vision, the Eye of Certainty

When you love God, the Prophet ﷺ and your shaykh so much that you can almost see them and feel their presence, this devotion

---

[206] These are the technical terms of Sufism, respectively, *'Ilm al-yaqeen* (Quran Suratu 't-Takaththur [The Piling Up], 102:5), *'Ayn al-yaqeen* (Suratu 't-Takaththur, 102:7), and *Haqqu 'l-yaqeen* (Suratu 'l-Waqi'ah [The Event], 56:95 and Suratu 'l-Haqqah [The Reality], 69:51).

[207] The Sufi technical terms are respectively, *Mahabbat ash-shaykh, Mahabbat an-Nabi, Mahabbatullah.*

[208] The Sufi technical terms are respectively *Hudurullah, Hudur al-Habib, Hudur ash-Shaykh.*

will lead you through the Reality of Hearing and the Reality of Vision until you reach the Truth of Certainty. Also known as the Truth of Reality, the Truth of Certainty is the "reality of reality." It is the station where there are no more changes based on perception. At this level, you understand the importance of the Qur'anic verse, *"Hold tight to the rope of God and do not separate."* This refers not merely to people, even though today's translations refer to this literal and basic meaning. On a deeper level it can be translated as, "Hold tight to real existence and do not separate from God's Presence, the Prophet's ﷺ presence and the presence of saints."

At this level, you know the importance of holding onto them, maintaining their presence. You would be willing to leave everything of this world to stay in their presence. Good tidings belong to those who, by riding upon their egos, have entered that reality. With such peace and tranquility, their followers are brought along.

At times this may appear to be a beautiful dream, but it is not a dream for those who are on this journey. Those who are not earnestly seeking, are like children who try to climb the first step and cannot. They try again and cannot, and yet again. Those who sincerely dedicate themselves to seeking will reach a level where they see, and the shaykh's treasures will be opened to them, the Prophet ﷺ treasures will be opened to them and finally, God's treasures will be opened to them as well.

Holding on to the rope of God is like holding on to a strong tree, of immense size. As you climb and reach the top, you can see from that height everything below you. You must know that nothing can move that tree, and you must try to emulate that condition. Fall comes and the tree sheds its leaves, followed by spring when new leaves spring forth. When you become firm and unwavering like that tree, God will grant you spiritual cycles of life similar to the tree's, where old knowledge goes and new knowledge comes. As much as you climb, you will be given more and more.

*We raise to degrees (of wisdom) whom We please: but*
*over all endued with knowledge is one, the All-*
*Knowing.*[209]

This verse may also be translated as, "above every knower is another knower." The ultimate "knower" may be interpreted as another person, rather than God. Above every knower is a knower, and you can ascend without limits, until you reach a state of bliss. There you will reach the saints, and the presence of Prophet Muhammad ﷺ.

Remember the importance of association with saints and do not separate from them. When you separate from them you are separating from those referred to in the following verse:

*All who obey God and the Apostle are in the company of*
*those on whom is the Grace of God - of the prophets (who*
*teach), the sincere (lovers of Truth), the witnesses (who*
*testify), and the Righteous (who do good): Ah! what a*
*beautiful fellowship!*[210]

When you *"hold tight and do not separate"* from the association of saints, you will never fall down, because they are there to pull you up. When they pull you up, you will achieve the level of being a disciple and all the remarkable realities that level holds. It is the Station of Self-Control, so try to hold yourself from falling into sins and mistakes. By holding tight to the association of saints, you will reach the eighth level.

---

[209] Surah Yusuf [Joseph], 12:76.
[210] Suratu 'n-Nisa [Women], 4:69.

$$\text{الفرار الى الله}$$

## 8. RUNNING TO GOD (*AL-FIRARU IL-ALLAH*)

*Hasten ye then (at once) to God. I am from Him a*
*Warner to you, clear and open![211]*

Go quickly, run to reach the Divine Presence. You are already inside. You are in that association of saints, in the Divine Presence.

You people, who are coming still seeking the way, run to God. This is the real way, the way of happiness, which is why saints ask their followers to run with them. When we are in the presence of our shaykhs, they speak of the afterlife. In fact, all their talk is of the afterlife.

They are dropping this world from their aim.

God is the Absolutely Perfect One. Everything He creates, He creates in absolute perfection. This entire universe, and whatever God has created other than it, are utterly flawless. Everything is symmetric to the ultimate detail, from the most colossal galaxy to the tiniest subatomic particle.

> *He Who created the seven heavens one above another:*
> *No want of proportion wilt thou see in the Creation of*
> *(God) Most Gracious. So turn thy vision again: seest*
> *thou any flaw?[212]*

So too, the creation of human beings is in complete perfection.

---

[211] Suratu 'dh-Dhariyat [The Winnowing Winds], 51:50.
[212] Suratu 'l-Mulk [Dominion], 67:3.

God engraved each human being in the best image to fit his or her personal nature. Imagine how stunned biologists are when they see how perfectly everything is functioning inside the brain's most essential component, an organ smaller than a lentil inside each person's head, similar in function to the microprocessor chip in a computer. That tiny organ is like an intricately-detailed computer chip, directing every aspect of mind and body, communicating with every organ and coordinating the actions of the trillions of cells that make up the body.

When they study this system doctors and scientists are astonished. The whole system of the body is governed by that minute lentil-size "chip" embedded in the brain. And every individual has a different program in his or her "chip." For computers, each different brand is programmed with a different software operating system, and no computer is the same. The human race consists of billions of human beings appearing from the time of the father of mankind Sayyidina Adam ﷺ, up to Judgment Day. In our time alone, humankind numbers six billion. That means there are six billion "chips," each one different from the other, and each chip has been programmed to function specifically for the human being in which it "runs."

That "chip" is placed in the most vital part of the body—the head. No one walks on his head, for God preserved it for these special functions. There He placed vision, hearing, smell, taste and touch. Within it he placed the mind, intellect, thought, reason and imagination.

Even the individual organs that compose the head are amazing in their function. Scientists who study the eyes are astounded at how they see, for their workings are utterly beyond even today's incredibly sophisticated technology; for the eye cannot be imitated. Each eye is filled with hundreds of thousands of minute nerves, each one far finer than a hair, with the blood flowing through them in parallel micro-arteries, all bundled together not unlike optical cables. God positioned the eyes and "wired" them, like spaceships and satellites, that sometimes contain millions of miles of wires. Within our body there are millions of miles of capillaries and nerves, finer than hairs, and everything is controlled by that tiny "chip" in the brain. That "chip" is so essential, that if it fails to function the person will go into a coma. When some people go into a coma doctors are able to "reboot" their "chip" and they come back. Others continue on their way to their Lord.

God said, "I want the most essential part of the body, that precious organ, the head, which contains the ears, the eyes, the mouth, the nose and the brain to be dedicated to Me." "That head," God says, "belongs to Me; I own all of it. And I want you to demonstrate to Me My greatness and My Lordship by bowing to me and making prostration to Me."

The head is obliged to make obeisance to the Lord. In truth our Lord honored us with the prostration, to demonstrate without a doubt, "You, our Lord, are our Master and we are Your servants."

It is for that reason that God made all the angels to bow down to Adam in the prostration of respect, to demonstrate to them that He has honored human beings, and has made them higher than the angels.[xviii]

On the night of Ascension, when the Prophet ﷺ was brought into the Divine Presence, where he observed God's utter absolute Greatness, he saw himself nothing. He felt that despite all of God's Grace, in granting to him to be the final messenger and the only one to ascend to the Divine Presence in his physical body, he saw himself as "indeed I am but a mere mortal like you," in the presence of his Lord.

If Prophet Muhammad ﷺ felt so humbled, then what about us? We must seek to be like that. Unfortunately arrogance, pride and anger consume us. We are overwhelmed by the seventeen ruinous traits and nothing results except fighting and abuse between people: brother against brother, brother against sister, sister against sister, husband against wife, children against parents, tribes, nations and continents, all fighting one another. Human beings have forgotten that they are servants of the same

Lord. We continue to see ourselves as great, important and deserving high regard. Despite this God created us to be happy, saying:

*We have honored the children of Adam.*[213]

That comes with a condition: seek His forgiveness and repent to Him. That is all that God asks. We cannot cease sinning, arguing and fighting, for we were created weak. "I only ask," God says, "when you realize your mistake, turn back to Me."

Therefore, when you realize your wrong, fall prostrate before God and seek His mercy and forgiveness, for when we go into prayer and that position of submission to God, then He is happy with us as His devoted servants.

"Run to God" means run to perfection. To perfect yourself is to achieve the state of *Ihsan*, as described in the famous Prophetic Tradition of the archangel Gabriel, we cited earlier:

*Ihsan is to worship God as if you see Him, and, since you cannot see Him, know that He sees you.*

To achieved that state of Perfection, one must first pass through the two preceding states: Islam, submission and *Iman*, faith.

Islam is the state of accepting the outward forms of the religion, its obligations and actions.

*Iman*, faith, is to accept not only the obligations, but it is to believe in God, the angels, God's books, His prophets, the Last Day and Destiny, both its good and its bad being from God most High.

Finally, *Ihsan*, is to perfect your ability to harmonize with other people, with the community, with your brothers and sisters, sons and daughter, father and mother, relations, friends and neighbors, with those of the same belief and with those possessing different beliefs. It means extending your hand to those who are different, helping them to understand yourself and the Way of

---

[213] Suratu 'l-Isra [The Night Journey], 17:70.

Islam. The perfected one is a diplomat, carrying the flag of spirituality in the best manner in order to demonstrate the highest levels of enlightenment and good conduct to all he encounters.

So running to perfection is as the Prophet ﷺ mentioned in the Prophetic Tradition of Archangel Gabriel ﷺ, running to God by worshipping Him as if you see Him. In order to see, you must run. As much as you run, you will taste from heavenly gnosticism, *ma'rifah*, sensing lights, angelic powers and heavenly scents and you will be adorned with all kinds of heavenly manners and ways of behavior that will cause you to run even faster towards that Divine Presence.

The Prophet ﷺ said, *"If you cannot see Him, know that He sees you"* for you are always under God's Mercy and Protection. When you achieve this level, God's guiding support, *inayah*, will reach you. This is known as the gentle Eastern wind, *reeh as-siba*, also known as the Breath of Youth, mentioned by Imam al-Busayri in his renowned poem *The Cloak* (*Qasidatu 'l-Burda*). As you advance in Gnostic levels, approaching God and the Prophet, they will carry you, as if on a magic carpet, from the depression of earthly burdens to an unlimited universe of perfection. Then you will become like a beacon of light, shining with every variety of color, penetrating veils of infinite knowledge. Then others can come to you and sip the taste of sweetness that comes in the bundles of different heavenly stars that are connected with that light that is granted to you through the Breath of Youth.

God said:

> *God is the light of the heavens and the earth. The example of His light is like a bundle; the bundle is in a glass and the glass is as if it were a shining star.*[214]

These are bundles of gnostic knowledge, *ma'rifah*. "Run to God" means run to His endless Oceans of Perfection; run to endless Oceans of Beauty; run to endless Oceans of Mercy; run to

---

[214] Suratu 'n-Nur [The Light], 24:35.

endless Oceans of Love; run to the endless Oceans of the Source of all sources.

# التمرين و التدبير

## 9. TRAINING (*AT-TAMRINU WA 'T-TADBIR*)

*And those who dispense their charity with their hearts*
*full of fear, because they will return to their Lord.*[215]

Just as you domesticate a wild horse, you have to domesticate and tame your ego. This is the ninth level, to fully control and ride your ego. At this level, it cannot ride you. Here the saints watch you. At this level great caution must be observed, for having achieved high levels and received immense openings, at this point Satan can begin to play with the seeker as he approaches his goal.

One of the first traps Satan will lay is to tell the aspiring seeker, "You are now a shaykh. You are free to do as inspiration comes to you."

Now you may claim to be a shaykh. However, even if forty shaykhs agree that someone is a shaykh, that person has no right to bring an innovation in religion. If he does, he is not a shaykh. Someone claiming to be a shaykh or a scholar—and a shaykh is higher, because a shaykh must first be a scholar—who claims that he is following the guidance of a teacher, and who considers himself to be an ascetic and one of the people of Sufism, such a person must be careful to avoid falling into the hands of Satan.

Satan may leverage that shaykh's bad desires so that he even begins to think about how to marry his disciples. It is not permissible to go to that extent, although you will see some

---

[215] Suratu 'l-Muminun [The Believer], 23:60.

187

shaykhs who consider themselves Sufis falling into this trap without concern for Islamic law. Under Islamic law there is permission to approach a woman with a marriage proposal. Today, however, there are shaykhs who are falling, failing to follow the legal means, because Satan is playing with them. Shaykhs or scholars have the right to marry whomever they like, but they must not have desire due to Satanic inspirations. When they give in to that way, they are falling completely into innovation. Such a shaykh must take an account of himself for what he is doing.

God said:

> And those who dispense their charity with their hearts
> full of fear, because they will return to their Lord ... [216]

At this level, disciples feel the fear of God. They are returning to Him and they are taming their egos, training them not to disobey their Lord, in accordance with this verse, and also:

> O ye who believe! Obey God, and obey the Messenger,
> and those charged with authority among you. If ye differ
> in anything among yourselves, refer it to God and His
> Messenger, if ye do believe in God and the Last Day:
> that is best, and most suitable for final determination.[217]

Most people spend more time making their egos happy than making God happy. The ego is happy with anything from this world, and is not happy with anything from the next world.

The Prophet ﷺ said:

> Everything with which a man plays is illusory, except for archery, learning to swim and horsemanship, because these are from Truth.

---

[216] Suratu 'l-Muminun [The Believer], 23:60.

[217] Suratu 'n-Nisa [Women], 4:59, also Cf. Suratu 'l-Ma'ida [The Spread Table], 5:92, Suratu 'n-Nur [The Light], 24:54, Surah Muhammad, 47:33, Suratu 't-Taghabun [Loss and Gain], 64:12.

According to this Tradition, we have permission to participate in sports. Beware however, of the ego's tricks. It will say to you concerning any sport, "No problem—this is for training." But this may be a trick to involve you in something that, in fact, detains and delays you, taking your time away from training your ego and performing your religious obligations. As a result, sports may give the ego an excuse to do what it likes from physical activity, rather than what is required. There may be no sin in sport, but it delays you from doing what you need to do.

Your ego does not recognize your shaykh, or scholars or anyone else for that matter. We have to fight the ego by training it to do what is essential. So, we begin to train the ego to speak truthfully, because that is what is most important. If you do not speak the truth, then you are lost.

Yahya bin Yahya asked Imam Malik for advice. Imam Malik told him:

> I will give you three pieces of advice. If you follow them you will be safe. My first advice is to speak truthfully, and if you do not know something admit it, and say, "I do not know."

Imam Malik told Yahya bin Yahya that all the knowledge he inherited from his 900 teachers—600 Sufi from Sufism and 300 from Islamic law—boiled down to this. It is the same truth that we referred to in the ninth level. This essential piece of advice, to say, "I do not know," brings your self down, and trains your ego to speak truthfully.

Among scholars, everyone wants to show that he has the most knowledge. Once, I was with Mawlana Shaykh Nazim ق and my uncle, who was extremely knowledgeable in teaching Maliki, Shafi'i and Hanafi jurisprudence. We were sitting with some scholars, and I asked my uncle to let Shaykh Nazim ق speak. My uncle looked at Mawlana, and Shaykh Nazim ق looked at my uncle. Mawlana Shaykh Nazim ق did not speak. Later he explained, saying, "Do not throw diamonds at the feet of children. It is meaningless to speak about wisdom there, because everyone wants to show his ego and pride, and no one will listen to what I have to say. Therefore, it is not necessary to speak."

Returning to the teaching of Imam Malik, he then said:

The second piece of advice that I will give you boils down all of the knowledge of physicians, all of the fruits of medicine, into one sentence: Do not eat until you are too full.[218]

This relates to the teaching of the Prophet ﷺ that the stomach is the "house of illness." He also said, "We are a people who do not eat until we get hungry, and when we eat we do not eat until we are full." If you follow this advice, you will never see sickness in your life. `

Imam Malik continued:

The third piece of advice I will give you is the essence of all wisdom: If you are among people, keep silent. If they reach a decision, it is as if it was your decision and as if you said what was necessary; if they make a mistake and you kept quiet, no one will blame you.

Imam Malik gave these three wisdoms in three phrases: speak the truth (saying "I do not know," if that is correct); do not eat too much; and be silent. By doing these things you will be training your ego as a man trains a horse for riding. When you ride the ego, it will not be controlling you. When you tell it, "I am not eating," it will say, "I hear and obey." However, if you are not training your ego, it will overcome you.

On the other hand, if I give you soup when you do not want to eat, that also goes against the ego's desire. The Way, *Tariqah*, means opposition to the all of the ego's desires. Therefore, you must eat if the shaykh orders you to do so. If the shaykh says, "Eat the whole pot of soup," you must finish it. How many times did Grandshaykh 'Abd Allah make us eat and eat and eat, until we

---

[218] literally, "up to your nose."

had to make more room for ourselves? In such situations, do not say, "Enough!" He is making that food with his supplications and prayers, and you are showing disobedience if you say, "No, I cannot eat anymore; it is enough." That is a test. Eating is not going to kill you. What if he orders you to a real challenge? If your shaykh says to eat, eat. Do not say, "No."

I never forgot the time that Grandshaykh 'Abd Allah al-Fa'iz ad-Daghestani ق gave old meat to my brother and me. In the old days, there were no refrigerators. People used to hang meat in the sun and in cabinets; when they wanted to eat it, they would boil it. So one time we were with him, about to return to Lebanon, and he said, "Do not go until you eat." Then he told his wife to go and get some meat. That whole house and kitchen was filled with a stench from the meat that she brought. Can you raise your head at such a time? No.

They brought the pot and put it in front of Grandshaykh 'Abd Allah ق. He took all the meat in big chunks and put it in a bowl. Oh, how it smelled! Who knows how many years that meat had been sitting in the closet? That was a test. It appeared as if he was going to poison us. Then he told us to eat. We looked, and could not eat. We saw thousands of maggots coming from the meat and from the bones. Mawlana Shaykh Nazim ق was looking and saying, "Eat!" But how could we eat?

We were nauseated to the point of almost vomiting. Everything was threatening to come out, but we knew that if we vomited we would be thrown out of *tariqah*. Grandshaykh 'Abd Allah ق was taking one big chunk into his mouth and it was gone, and another chunk—gone. We readied water to quickly wash down this horrific, rotten meat, then with, "*Bismillahi 'r-Rahmani 'r-Rahim*," we began to eat. As soon as we put the meat in our mouths, the smell was gone and the worms disappeared.

Shaykhs want to check you. They create an entire scene in front of your eyes to train you. They perfect you, and then they give you from the trust they hold for you.

الاستماع

## 10. LISTENING (*AL-ISTIMA'*)

*If God had found in them any good, He would indeed*
*have made them listen; (As it is) if He had made them*
*listen, they would but have turned back and declined*
*(Faith).*[219]

When your ego is trained to obey, at the tenth and final step, how
do you obey? Through listening. If the ego is good, it will listen,
but God knows that the bad ego will never listen unless it is
trained and controlled.

When the ego is riding you, it will never listen. Rather, you
will listen to it—even though it might tell you to leave your
family, your friends or even your community. You do not hear
anything else. That is why the verse says that God would have
made them listen if they had any good in them. God knows they
are not going to listen, since the ego is riding on them. When the
ego is in control, you will not listen.

However, at the last level, when you have left everything and
reached the level of "hearing and obeying," you will have trained
your ego to be ridden. Then you will say:

*We hear and obey; forgive us, O Lord, and You are the*
*ultimate destination.*[220]

---

[219] Suratu 'l-Anfal [The Spoils of War], 8:23.
[220] Suratu 'l-Baqara [The Cow], 2:285.

That is the highest level, the power of listening. The Prophet ﷺ exemplifies two levels: listening and obeying. He listened to Jibril ﷺ, who brought the message, and he delivered it. The highest level of Islam is found in *tariqah*. That is found after all the nine levels we described have been passed. That level is listening, accepting everything, obeying, repenting and going to our Lord.

There are four different stages to listening:

The first stage of this tenth level is to go from unbelief to faith. That is the highest goal—not to associate anything with God and to believe in Him.

The second stage is to go from disobedience and sin to obedience.

The third stage is to leave innovation for the practice of the Prophet ﷺ, the Sunnah.

The fourth stage is to leave heedlessness for awareness. All four of these stages are subcategories of listening.

The Prophet ﷺ said, *"To regret is to repent."*[221] While forbidden in Islam, in the preceding prophets' communities, God never accepted the repentance of the Children of Israel unless they killed themselves. That is why Prophet Moses ﷺ ordered the repenting followers of as-Samiri to kill themselves. He returned from his seclusion and found them worshipping the Golden Calf and following as-Samiri, and in order to repent they had to die.

> *And remember Moses said to his people: "O my people!*
> *Ye have indeed wronged yourselves by your worship of*
> *the calf: So turn (in repentance) to your Maker, and slay*
> *yourselves (the wrong-doers); that will be better for you*
> *in the sight of your Maker." Then He turned towards*
> *you (in forgiveness): For He is Oft-Returning, Most*
> *Merciful.*[222] xix

---

[221] Ahmad and al-Hakim in his *Mustadrak*.
[222] Suratu 'l-Baqara [The Cow], 2:54.

For the community of Prophet Muhammad ﷺ, it is different. God said:

> ... *And O ye Believers! turn ye all together towards God,*
> *that ye may attain Bliss.*[223]

The Prophet ﷺ said, *"Repent, for I ask repentance seventy times every day."*[224] In some versions, he said, "one hundred times." That is why, in the daily Naqshbandi liturgy, we repeat "God forgive us - *Astaghfirullah*" seventy times. The Prophet ﷺ also said:

> *The one who repents from his sins becomes like one who never*
> *sinned at all.*[225]

Repentance is obligatory on every Muslim, non-Muslim, male, female, sick person and healthy person, whether stationary or traveling. There is no question about it—it is obligatory for everyone.

You might work on some of these levels at the same time, but you must complete the first step in order to take the second, and so on. That is why saints order seclusion to disciples. In seclusion, they can progress through the levels from one to ten, without jumping up and down. If you jump up and down you might break a leg.

---

[223] Suratu 'n-Nur [The Light], 24:31.
[224] Bukhari.
[225] Ibn Majah.

# الحقائق القلبية الست

## THE SIX POWERS OF THE HEART
### AL-HAQA'IQ AL-QALBIYYAH AS-SITT

# THE OPENING OF THE HEART

Having attained the level of disciple, the seeker knows the Truth of Certainty. When the Saints of God witness that the seeker has reached enlightenment by passing the ten steps to discipleship, they will dress him or her with six powers. These are not powers that come from an external source, but rather they are unveiled from within the heart of the disciple. When they are opened, he will find himself dressed with them.

A light may be entirely concealed within a room that has no opening to the outside. However, if a door or window is opened, the light shines forth. If the room is filled with light, light will come out. If it is filled with smoke, smoke will come out.

Imagine that a piece of burning coal is placed with a great quantity of incense inside a container. If the container is small and the heat very intense, the fragrance of perfume erupts like a volcano when the container is opened. When a volcano erupts, it explodes up in the air hundreds of feet, spreading lava and ash everywhere, taking everything with it. A similar reaction occurs in the heart of a disciple after he passes the ten levels. His heart is that small container with a fire burning inside. The perfumed lava is the love that rose in him from the Love of God, the Prophet ﷺ and the shaykh—the love that comes from annihilation in them. The intensity of the love in his heart and the immensity of the six powers in his heart explode into his surroundings, releasing that lava of love upon everything he touches.

By permission of the Saints of God, and especially the shaykhs of the distinguished Naqshbandi Order, these powers appear and thus many miracles may be performed. However, the shaykhs do not approve of showing miracles. They do not like to show off.

They conserve divine blessings in order to help others, either in an indirect way, or in the grave during the angelic questioning. At that point, when the angels ask such questions as "Who is your Lord?" and "Who is your prophet?" the disciple trembles with fear. Then the Naqshbandi shaykh uses the Divine Power God has granted to him to loosen the student's tongue, so that he can give the correct answer. That is when the student needs the shaykh the most. He will also need the shaykh to present him to the Prophet Muhammad 🌸 as his follower, and to request the Prophet's intercession for him. Only true saints have access to the Prophet 🌸. Not everyone has access. Those who have access to the Prophet 🌸 take their miracles to him, and so the disciples of the Naqshbandi shaykhs are prevented from outwardly displaying their power. Other orders are different; they have their own way.

If these six powers of the heart are suppressed by the bad characteristics of the ego, they will never be released. The ego's selfishness cannot accept anyone except itself, not even the shaykh.

*Saying, "I am your Lord, Most High".* [226]

The ego's ultimate aim is to overthrow God's dominion of the heart and for the ego to proclaim itself as lord. The ego wants to ride and control you, and it is able to suppress these powers in your heart. You cannot release them until you pass the ten steps of the disciple. Then it is as if you have been granted the highest level of clearance, for each of the ten steps is like a new level of security clearance.

For certain government services, you require security clearance. For example, while most people who work in the Department of Labor do not need such clearance because their regular duties are not sensitive in nature, many of those in the Department of Defense do. Without such clearance, you may only access unclassified areas. High-level government jobs require high

---

[226] Suratu 'n-Nazi'at [Those Who Pull Out], 79:24.

levels of clearance. Applicants must be examined carefully before receiving this high-level clearance. Their family history and criminal records are examined, along with anything else that might make the candidate a risk. This information affects the level of clearance they are eligible to receive. Depending on the level of clearance, this research might go back as far as the age of five years.

The same is true in spirituality. When the disciple has achieved these ten levels, he is cleared to access classified materials. At that time, the disciple can access the six powers of the heart, powers that are found in the heart of every human being, without discrimination. Until you access them, these six powers are pressurized by the ego. The tyranny of the self is able to oppress you. All of this power that God put in your heart becomes suppressed in a small and narrow place, due to the very high pressure of selfishness and satanic influence. The pressurized place that holds these powers is a black clot in the heart.[xx] When you have achieved clearance through progress, that place becomes easy to open. When that pressurized clot is opened, it is like aerosol releasing a nice fragrance. Like the volcano, the heart containing these powers erupts, spreading love.

The six powers are of the heart are:

- ❖ The Reality of Attraction (*Haqiqatu 'l-jadhbah*)
- ❖ The Reality of Downpouring (*Haqiqatu 'l-fayd*)
- ❖ The Reality of Focusing (*Haqiqatu 't-tawajjuh*)
- ❖ The Reality of Intercession (*Haqiqatu 't-tawassul*)
- ❖ The Reality of Guidance (*Haqiqatu 'l-irshad*)
- ❖ The Reality of Scrolling (*Haqiqatu 't-tayy*)

Every newborn child has these six powers, because every child is born innocent. The light of innocence is lost throughout life. God does not take it away; it is suppressed and pushed down into the heart as the child grows progressively farther away from his divine reality. A child may be raised by his parents in a situation contrary to his inherent innocence (*fitrah*). How severe the suppression of this light becomes depends on how the child is raised and how much the child is spoiled. As the child grows into adulthood, he or she may suddenly realize the importance of balancing the inner and outer dimension of his life, in order to release the spiritual power buried within them.

Maintaining balance becomes an integral part of the seeker's discipline. It is very important to have the inward and the outward in harmony. A person's outer behavior must match their inner reality, or else the six powers cannot be opened. In that case, they will continue to struggle.

When someone tries to disguise the disparity between their inner and outer realities, they make their outward demeanor appear noble to others. That person may claim to have permission to represent a saint and give guidance, or they may claim to have had a dream and received permission from the Prophet ﷺ to guide people. Others may say, "I don't need a dream. I received permission by direct telepathy from the Prophet ﷺ to give guidance to people." These are people whose pride and arrogance forces them to pretend they are leaders. Everyone has a different ego problem, but these are examples of polishing one's outside while the inside remains bad. Such a person is a hypocrite and a liar. He is like someone whose inner core is iron, completely dark and cold, but who coats it with silver. That person has a heart that is silver-plated. If you knew that, you would never buy what he is selling. You would discard it because you would then know that you had been cheated. Others look and buy it because they are fooled and think that what is only silver-plated is really silver.

How many shaykhs do we have like that around the world today, pretending to be something they are not? They are going to be questioned by God about how they cheated and deceived people. That is why a shaykh must be very careful to always say, "I am nothing." If you do not know about something, admit that you do not know.

There was once was a son of a great shaykh who, when his father died, began to also don the garb of a shaykh so that everyone would come to him for advice. He never admitted, "I am not a scholar." When people would come to him with a problem, he would nod his head as if contemplating the answer and say, "hmmm." The student would wait and then ask, "What is the answer, O shaykh?" He usually responded, "There are two opinions on that." Everyone was impressed by this answer and would never bother to find out what those two opinions were. They would hear this and go. However, one of the clever ones knew that the man was a charlatan. He asked the man a question in front of others, to which he gave his usual response, saying again, "There are two opinions." This time, however, the answer exposed him, for the question that had been put to him was, "Is there any doubt in God's existence?"

This is an example of the state of scholars today. Do not fall into that trap of lying, or being a hypocrite. Do not be silver-plated, or you will be lost. Do not give lectures on the love of the Prophet ﷺ or on remembrance of the Divine when, in reality, you know nothing about these things. So many are like this; do not be fooled.

While the silver-plated person has an inner identity that is ugly, but maintains a nice exterior, there also people who do everything they can to clean their inner-selves, but who fail to improve their external appearance. Such a person may say, "I know that my appearance is ugly, but what can I do? At least my inner character is good. I do not lie. I might make mistakes, but I am careful not to do anything wrong." This person has an interior that is silver, and an exterior that is iron. He is iron-plated. He is humble, and he does not cheat. He says, "I belong with the shoes that are left at the door. I know nothing."

However, the best people are those who have polished their interior and their exterior completely. Such a person is one of the Veracious ones (siddiq). That person is not even like silver, but is like gold—inwardly and outwardly unchanging. That is the perfect one. That is what you achieve when you move through these ten steps of discipleship, clearing one level and then another, and manage to make your inner and outer realities equal. At that time, the volcano of the heart erupts to release the six powers, and the fragrance of them comes out. As soon as you smell this fragrance, you begin to see what people cannot see and hear what people cannot hear. By smelling the fragrance of a flower, the bee can travel very great distances to reach what it needs and return. What makes the bee unique is that it receives inspiration, unlike any other creature.[227] When the fragrance of the six powers opens, all kinds of inspiration will come to you and these powers will dress your external reality.

---

[227] *And thy Lord inspired the bee...* Suratu 'n-Nahl [The Bee], 16:68.

## DECODING THE REALITIES

The six powers in the heart of the disciple must be decoded by passing the ten levels. A message must be decoded before its information can be read. In spirituality, there are many encoded messages, because we are always confusing messages through our bad actions. To reach the reality of these messages requires decoding. These messages are within the heart, but we have to be able to unlock them.

Once a student came to Sayyidina Bayazid ق and said, "O my shaykh. I was following you all my life. I was learning from you all my life. I never missed an association (*suhbat*). I never missed a session for remembrance (*dhikr*). I never missed a prayer. I served you with sincerity and piety, but I am not able to understand these six realities that you are speaking about. I am not seeing them and I am not feeling them."

Sayyidina Bayazid ق said, "O my son, if you worship 300 years—let alone fifty years—you will never reach these realities, as long as you are carrying your ego with you."

The disciple asked, "O my shaykh, is there a cure to let go of that ego?"

The Shaykh said, "Of course, if you are willing to follow that cure."

He said, "Please, tell me quickly in order that I will be able to cure myself."

Sayyidina Bayazid al-Bistami ق looked at him, and said, "O my son, in order to get rid of this sickness—and there is no one without it—you have to hang a bag around your neck and fill it with walnuts. Go to where everyone knows you, downtown where the scholars congregate. Go with these walnuts and say, 'O children of the community, I love you so much. Come. To anyone who slaps my face, I will give one walnut. Anyone who slaps me twice will get two walnuts.'"

This was to humiliate him, to bring his ego down. That disciple was a great scholar, and he was acting according to what he knew. But there are two different types of knowledge: the knowledge of paper and the knowledge of taste. They are very different from each other, the difference between reading about something and really tasting it. Someone who studies medicine must have an internship in order to understand what he has learned from books.

The disciple looked at his shaykh, not believing what he was hearing. He said to his shaykh, "*Subhanallah!* Glory be to God! Can you say something like this to someone like me?" By this statement, he meant, "I am a great scholar; everyone knows me." The shaykh said, "Stop! You are committing idolatry (*shirk*) by praising God in reference to yourself." For the scholar it was as if the thought of humiliating himself was such an amazement beyond the imagination- comparable to God's wondrous power and creation.

How far we are from the Truth! How far we are from knowing ourselves! The Prophet ﷺ said:

*Whoever knows himself, knows his Lord.*[228]

Make an account of yourself and see if you have this sickness or not. How much ego everyone is carrying! No one can accept anything from anyone else. The ego is difficult, giving itself excuses.

Once there was a student of Sayyidina Jamaluddin al-Ghumuqi al-Husayni ق named Orkallisa Muhammad who spent all his life trying to please his shaykh and be a good follower. He learned how to behave with the shaykh from the preceding story of Sayyidina Bayazid al-Bistami ق and his disciple.

---

[228] al-Zarkashi in *al-Tadhkira*, and al-Suyuti in *al-Durar al-Muntathira*.

One night, after making *dhikr* and praying the night prayer, everyone left and the mosque was closed. But Orkallisa Muhammad had hidden himself inside, behind a pillar. He was speaking to himself, like someone who speaks to his reflection in a mirror. In this dialogue, it was as if the body had one voice and the spirit another.

He said, "O Orkallisa Muhammad, you were never able to do anything. You always fail at what you touch. You failed and failed, until finally the shaykh pitied you and gave you money to buy a flock of sheep. You bought so many sheep and raised them until the sacred months arrived, but with every holiday in those months you sacrificed them in the Way of God until none were left. Your shaykh gave you money for the sheep in order for you to earn an income to help the community, but you went and slaughtered them all, and so you failed. Whatever the shaykh gives you to do, you fail."

He was learning. He knew his self—the self that will destroy human beings. Never trust yourself and let it ride on you; you must ride on your self.

He continued, "O Orkallisa Muhammad, I make an oath that you are the worst of human beings, the lowest that anyone can imagine." To show the sincerity of his oath, he added, "If I am not saying this with full conviction that I am the worst human being, then my beloved wife is divorced from me."

With that oath, he was experiencing the reality of humility. He was genuinely accepting that he was the worst of human beings. At that moment, he heard his shaykh laughing, and he looked up and saw him. He said, "O my shaykh, you are here?"

Sayyidina Jamaluddin ق replied, "I was here from the beginning, O my son. Now I can open for you the six powers that are in your heart."

Today, you have the Palm Pilot, and with its stylus you are able to bring up the information it holds. Such a stylus is not the same instrument that Sayyidina Jamaluddin al-Ghumuqi al-Husayni ق was using, but technology imitates the abilities of spiritual teachers. By moving the Finger of Witnessing in front of the heart of the disciple, the shaykh opened the six realities for him. He was uploading, bringing that information up into the awareness of the disciple. As that information was being decoded, the disciple was ascending and descending in the mosque. He was so very light, for heavenly powers were raising him.

The disciple said, "Is this part of the spiritual path?"

The shaykh replied, "Yes it is, but this does not come to someone until he humbles himself. If he keeps thinking that he is something, then he will never reach the reality that he is asking to learn."

The taste of this world is going to vanish. When someone is in the grave, after some time the body decomposes. Thus, the taste of this world is also not going to stay forever. Those who try to taste from this world are moved by its difficulties and its temporary pleasures. In reality, it is only a rotting corpse that every dog is trying to take a bite from. This is our situation. Everyone now is fighting for this world.

The saints of God are fighting to reach the next world. In this world, they want the satisfaction of God. Others want the pleasure of the afterlife but they want to get it in this world. Instead of preparing for the next world, they are running after this world and finding its difficulties. When we run after the next world, these six powers will open in our hearts. However, as long as we run after this world, those realities remain rooted in the heart and never open, since they have not been decoded.

حقيقة الجذبة

# 1. THE REALITY OF ATTRACTION
## (*HAQIQATU 'L-JADHBAH*)

*"Yet when the Servant of God stands forth to invoke
Him, they just make round him a dense crowd."*[229]

The Reality of Attraction is like a magnet, and the magnet's power depends upon how much gold has been achieved in your heart, how much fragrance was contained in your heart and how much of it you are able to release. Some disciples can carry more and some carry less, but all will be given that power. Sayyidina Muhammad al-Busiri ق said that either you are taking from the waters of the Prophet ﷺ with your palm or with a pitcher. This power of attraction is not really how many people are attracted to you, but how much you are attracted to the Prophet ﷺ, and if you are taking handfuls of knowledge or pitchers of knowledge from him as a true gnostic. As your attraction to that knowledge increases, so do your efforts to bring it from the Prophet's heart to yours. This knowledge never ends; as saints are taking from the ocean of the Prophet ﷺ, the Prophet ﷺ is taking from the Divine name the Knower (*al-'Alim*).

*And above every knower is a higher knower.* [230]

Before the opening of this power, why should people be attracted to you? Should they be attracted because you are this or

---

[229] Suratu 'l-Jinn [The Jinn], 72:19.
[230] Surah Yusuf [Joseph], 12:76.

206

you are that, holding a position in this world? The attraction of such people is not the Reality of Attraction; it is an imitation of the real power that God gives to his servants for their followers. The attraction given to worldly figures is like a plastic fruit, with no taste. What you see may be attractive, but it is tasteless.

The attraction of the saints of God is for the Prophet ﷺ, who dresses them with a beautiful fragrance. Because you partake of that fragrance, the eyes of the Prophet ﷺ will be on you. The mosque should be a place for the best ornaments, and one of the most important ornaments that you use when you go to the mosque is perfume.

The Prophet ﷺ said:

*Lovely to me are three things from your world: women, beautiful fragrance, and the refreshment of my eyes in prayer.*[231]

Through the Prophet's love for them, God has honored women. They are the ones undergoing so much difficulty in this life, and they are the first to enter paradise in the afterlife by the intercession of the Prophet ﷺ. This is not the place to go deeply into interpretation, because the sayings of the Prophet ﷺ can carry millions of meanings, just as in the Holy Qur'an, each verse can carry billions of meanings. Understanding depends upon how much you are inheriting from the knowledge of the Prophet.

"Prayer" is not from this world; it is from the Next World. But the Prophet ﷺ included it in this world to show that it is a means for his Community to be in a better position on Judgment Day.

What do "women" symbolize, if not beauty? When the Prophet ﷺ includes women, he is describing the Manifestation of beauty (*Tajalli al-jamal*). God dressed the Prophet ﷺ with the Reality of beauty (*Haqiqatu 'l-jamal*), the appearance of His Attributes.

The Prophet said:

---

[231] Ahmad Ibn Hanbal, an-Nasa'ee, Ibn Sa'd's *Tabaqat*.

*God is beautiful and He loves beauty.*[232]

When the Prophet ﷺ says, "I love women," it means that he loves beauty. That is why saints often pray, "O God, allow us to marry the women of Paradise." They are asking to be dressed by God's Beauty, to which the beauty of the inhabitants of Paradise cannot compare. The Prophet ﷺ went to the mosque dressed by His Beautiful Attributes, with beautiful characteristics.

Beautiful fragrance is from a heavenly source, and the highest fragrance is in the heart. The perfume that is pressurized in the heart is beautiful, and it is that fragrance that the Prophet ﷺ was dressed with when he went to the mosque to pray.

When the Station of Attraction is opened, this beauty will begin to appear on you; the fragrance blowing from the heart like a volcano will ornament you, and then you will attract the sight of the Prophet. We say, *"Give us a glance from your vision, (O Messenger of God)."*[233] A glance from him turns the sinner into one who repents, and raises you higher and higher. The Prophet ﷺ can do this because he was given Intercession. If he sees goodness, he praises God, and if he sees otherwise, he asks forgiveness.

When you bring a magnet to a nail, the nail is attracted. You are a nail, nothing more than that. There are silver-plated nails today, like plastic professors and lecturers, and there are those neither silver-plated nor gold-plated, but pure gold; all are nails. When you pass the ten levels, you become a magnet, like the nail that has been rubbed by a magnet becomes a magnet.

Prophet Muhammad ﷺ said:

*When a group of people sit in a gathering to remember God, then His mercy covers them.*[234]

Who is His Mercy, mentioned in this Prophetic Tradition? God called Sayyidina Muhammad ﷺ the Forgiving, Merciful one,

---

[232] Muslim.

[233] Suratu 'n-Nisa [Women], 4:46.

[234] Muslim.

*Ra'ufun, Rahim.*[235] He gave him the power to look at people, and that is why saints stand up when Sayyidina Muhammad ﷺ is mentioned in a gathering. While some people say not to stand up, in reality we are obliged to stand up at every moment, as we would in the presence of his Noble Tomb. His description of mercy as covering people means not only that it surrounds and encompasses, but also that it rubs. When people are remembering God, angels are rubbing people and dressing them from their angelic attire, like a magnet rubbing a nail. Then, because of your fragrance and beauty, the Prophet ﷺ will look at you, and he will dress you with mercy. When he dresses you, you become someone who attracts others. You become a focal point to whom all are drawn, like a spotlight or searchlight, you become a beacon so that people can see. You become like a beacon that guides vessels in the ocean and in the air, a light in dark nights.

---

[235] Suratu 't-Tawbah, [Repentance] 9:108.

حقيقة الفيض

## 2. THE REALITY OF DOWNPOURING
### (*HAQIQATU 'L-FAYD*)

*And when they listen to the revelation received by the
Messenger, thou wilt see their eyes overflowing with
tears.*[236]

When you become a beacon, you must be filled with knowledge,
or else what kind of beacon will you be? You must be filled by the
reality of Downpouring, *Fayd*. Sometimes fog comes over a
mountain and is something that continuously moves, covering
everything. Such a fog is not something that stops; rather it is
always rolling and moving, rolling and moving. Some goes and
more comes. In South Africa there is a high mountain in Cape
Town where this may be seen. That is what is called *Fayd*, a rolling
power that descends from heavens.

If someone possesses the Reality of Divine Downpouring
(*Fayd al-ilahi*), there is more that comes than is already present,
and it is always coming. Knowledge (*'ilm*) is always coming. God
gave knowledge to the Prophet ﷺ – the Holy Qur'an. From the
Prophet's heart to the heart of the disciple will be sent the Divine
Downpouring; through his shaykh it will be dressing him, and he
will be raised higher and higher in knowledge. *"And above every
knower is a higher knower."* Where the disciple is raised depends
upon his level.

---

[236] Suratu 'l-Ma'idah [The Spread Table], 5:83.

The Downpouring increases our powers, and brings you, as Abu al-Hasan al-Shadhili ق said, to the level of someone who has dropped this world from his eyes, and looks only for the Next World. But the Downpouring doesn't come unless four manners are present:

1. Respect for elders (*al-hurmat li 'l-akabir*). Here "elders" means the Saints of God, those granted to be sages. You have to respect them. The literal meaning of "elders" is also present.

2. Mercy for the younger (*ar-rahmat li 'l-asaghir*). You have to have mercy for those who are beginners, and who are lovers. Do not have the look of superiority. Remember when Bayazid al-Bistami ق tested his disciples, and they all ran away, except for one. When Bayazid ق approached him, he said, "O my shaykh, I have prepared water for you." Sayyidina Bayazid ق said, "Where are your fellow disciples?" He said, "O my shaykh, I was busy for you; I did not notice." Do not belittle those who have love, or look at them with disgust, but respect them.

3. Be fair to yourself (*al-insaf min nafsih*). Be fair in blaming yourself. If your ego did something wrong, you have to punish yourself. If your ego made a mistake, you must make it go without eating and drinking, so that the next day it will not make the same mistake.

4. Never give yourself an excuse (*'Adm al-intisari laha*). There is no excuse for the ego. You must bring the ego down always, to make sure it cannot dominate you.

To achieve the Divine Downpouring you have to carry these four manners.

God said to Prophet David ﷺ, "O David, say to My sincere servants not to see themselves as great or knowledgeable, for if I judge them with My Balance, I would punish them without being unjust."

The Prophet ﷺ said:

*If your sins reach to the sky and you repent God would forgive you.*

## 3. THE REALITY OF FOCUSING
### (*HAQIQATU 'T-TAWAJJUH*)

The Reality of Focusing is the secret of these verses:

*From whencesoever Thou startest forth, turn Thy face in
the direction of the sacred Mosque; that is indeed the
truth from the Lord. And God is not unmindful of what
ye do.* [237]

Wherever you are, you must direct your face towards the
Ka'ba; but this can be understood together with the verse:

*To God belong the East and the West: Whithersoever ye
turn, there is the presence of God. For God is all-
Pervading, all-Knowing.* [238]

So the Ka'ba is where you direct your face, and where God is
present. It is the most sacred mosque, where sins are prohibited.
The secret of directing your face (*sirru 't-tawajjuh*) is in focusing on
that place where no sin is going to be committed. The Reality of
Focusing means that you only direct your face where no one can
commit sins. It is forbidden to direct your face anywhere else.

You must be on a sacred journey at all times, as if you are
facing the Ka'ba, as if you are facing God. Your journey cannot be
on the television; it cannot be in movie theatres; it cannot be
accomplished by wasting time. If you desire to reach that reality,

---

[237] Suratu 'l-Baqara [The Cow], 2:149, 2:150.
[238] Suratu 'l-Baqara, 2:115.

if you want to say, "I am a disciple," then you must follow the way of the disciple. You cannot say, "I am a student," and then do whatever you like to do. Then you are a student who is ignorant (*jahl*), and knowledge (*'ilm*) is the opposite of ignorance.

In this world you are faced with choosing simple interest or compound interest. Loan sharks, all are cheating you. You are buying houses with compound interest, and so you may pay interest only for many years. There is also simple ignorance and compound ignorance. Simple ignorance is when you have ignorance of things, when you are ignorant in the affairs of life. If you are judged to be ignorant in business, in science, or in planting fields, does it really matter? Compound ignorance is when you are ignorant in the way of God, and that is dangerous. Compound ignorance accumulates, when sins upon sins are written for you. When you have compound ignorance, you know that you are doing something wrong, but still you insist on doing it. Simple ignorance relates only to this world. Your ignorance of how to make a chair does not count against you, but it is dangerous to not know how to pray.

When you have achieved the ten levels of discipleship, and the Realities of Attraction and of Downpouring are bestowed upon you, you are dressed with heavenly decorations like a rainbow of beautiful colors. Then God directs you to His Face. From any place, the Saints of God are seeing the Divine Presence, unlike common people.

With the Reality of Focusing, a person becomes a sign from among the Signs of God, a Sign of God moving upon the earth. When you move with that power, by directing yourself to God's Face, by His permission and power and by the Prophet's power and permission, you can reach anyone by telepathy, from heart to heart. Now dressed by God with that power, you may look after your followers, and guide them through their lives. Saints are ordered by a heavenly order coming from the Prophet ﷺ to look at their disciples at least three times a day, and when they look at you they have to navigate. Today you navigate the Internet. There are also saints navigating a heavenly Internet, directing their disciples wherever they want.

There are higher and higher examples of this power. When we were young, my brother and I had traveled from Beirut to Damascus to visit Grandshaykh 'Abd Allah al-Fa'izi Daghestani ق without our mother's permission, and the shaykh opened the door before we knocked, stopped us and turned us away. We ran from his majesty. We returned the next day with permission, and Grandshaykh sent his servant to open the door for us. The previous day he showed us that he knew we were coming. When we went in, he explained that when saints look at their disciples, they do not give them sweets to make them feel happy. To make someone happy is easy. They look at them to create difficulties for them. When disciples carry difficulties, saints take from them their burdens and make them clean. If they don't carry them, saints ask forgiveness on their behalf in order to clean them.

Every time you face a difficulty, it is like a puzzle. Be sure to say, "My shaykh is testing me now, my Prophet ﷺ is testing me now, God is testing me now. Now that my shaykh is looking at me, how will I keep myself?" Do not move like a windmill, which turns when the wind comes. Be like a pine tree; winter and summer it is green.

The ability to reach the first level of sainthood is given with the Reality of Focusing. At that time the Truth of Spirits (*Haqiqatu 'l-arwah*) can be reached, beyond the Truth of Hearts (*Haqiqatu 'l-qulub*) and the Truth of Secrets (*Haqiqatu 'l-asrar*). When the fragrance comes with the Reality of Downpouring, you can direct that beautiful fragrance. The shaykh is able to communicate with his disciple. The disciple will begin to have a receiver, and he will pick up with it where the shaykh is directing him, and undertake his journey *"to the presence of God"* and *"in the direction of the sacred Mosque."* When you reach the Reality of Focusing, you can communicate with anyone you want - without a cellular phone.

Fifty years ago, before phones were so readily available, I witnessed the famous Shaykh Ahmad Haroun of Damascus display this power. He was sitting with his followers, and needed something from one of his disciples in Aleppo, hundreds of miles away. Shaykh Ahmad Haroun unfastened his belt and lifted it to his mouth, and said, "Hello, I want you here. Bring the book that I need." Then he hung up his belt. Five hours later there was a knock. When the door was opened, that disciple was there. He said, "O my shaykh, you called me and I brought you the book."

How did Shaykh Ahmad Haroun do that? The disciple can hear the shaykh, and for shaykhs this communication is simple, as for us normal people today communicating by cell phones is so ordinary. Technology of today is following the spiritual technology that has been present in all human beings but is manifested in those who are trained and given permission to use it. You may have a cell phone but you need the cellular provider to give you access to the network, otherwise your phone is a useless piece of plastic. Once you have an agreement with one of these huge cellular companies you may begin to use their service. Similarly when the student is given initiation by the shaykh his chip is now linked to the shaykh's. When the shaykh activates the code more and more powers of the heart may be opened. Such wondrous powers may be seen throughout the centuries even dating back to the Companions of the Prophet. (as illustrated in the incident of 'Umar ibn al-Khattab ﷺ seeing and speaking all the way from Madina to Damascus in the chapter on the Reality of Scrolling described on page 220). However, saints do not value such things more than knowledge. Knowledge is more important.

## 4. THE REALITY OF INTERCESSION
### (*HAQIQATU 'T-TAWASSUL*)

*Who is there who can intercede in His presence except as
He permitteth?*[239]

*None shall have the power of intercession, but such a one
as has received permission from (God) Most Gracious.*[240]

When you are established in the power of focusing, the Saints of
God dress you with a higher power, the Reality of Intercession.
With this reality you can intercede for people, inheriting as much
of this secret as you can from the Prophet ﷺ. Your inheritance
depends upon your container. You may take as much as your
heart can carry, but all saints may take from a single drop. The
Prophet's intercession is so vast that one drop is like an ocean. It is
enough to drown the whole world. All saints are swimming in a
single drop of intercession. Think about how much power God
gave to the Prophet ﷺ for interceding on Judgment Day. We are
like babies in diapers.

You cannot understand the knowledge of the Saints of God,
how they are swimming in that drop. How are you going to
understand the reality of Prophet Muhammad ﷺ? Today, books
are written about the Prophet ﷺ, but they contain only the
"knowledge of papers" (*'ilm al-awraq*).

---

[239] Suratu 'l-Baqara [The Cow], 2:255.
[240] Surah Maryam [Mary], 19:87.

It is God's overwhelming Mercy that will suffice for humankind's salvation on the most dreaded day. And the embodiment of God's Mercy is the God Messenger Muhammad ﷺ, whom He described in the Holy Qur'an as:

*a Mercy for all creatures.* [241]

It is therefore our hope in the Prophet's ﷺ intercession that is our firmest foothold in the Hereafter, not dependence on deeds, whose sincerity and perfection are undoubtedly lacking. It is only through the Mercy of God, as perfectly embodied in the person of His Beloved Prophet ﷺ that we can rest assured of safety and deliverance:

*on the Day in which hearts and eyes will be*
*overturned.*[242]

The Prophet ﷺ said:

*I myself am the Beloved of God (*habibullah*) and I say this without pride, and I carry the flag of glory on the Day of Judgment and am the first intercessor and the first whose intercession is accepted...*[243]

And God's Messenger ﷺ said:

*My intercession is for the grave sinners of my community.* [244]

That power granted to the Prophet ﷺ is inherited by his spiritual successors, the saints (*awliyaullah*). The Reality of Intercession means that, in making prostration, the saint will not raise his head until his follower gains "clearance." A person working in government cannot see classified material without clearance. In spirituality, you need "clearance" to reach "classified" material. That "clearance" comes from being clean, and the shaykh cleans you in that prostration. In that prostration,

---

[241] Suratu 'l-Anbiya [The Prophets], 21:107
[242] Suratu 'n-Nur [The Light], 24:37.
[243] Tirmidhi.
[244] Tirmidhi.

they bring all their followers and present them clean to the Prophet ﷺ. For the saints of God, this is the reality of interceding for their followers.

God's Messenger ﷺ said:

*None amongst you can get into Paradise by virtue of his deeds alone.*[245]

Even the good deeds of the seekers on the Way require intercession, for due to our ignorance, whatever we perform of good actions is marred by many forms of wrongdoing, secreted within them. That is why intercession is also needed by the follower of a saint for every deed he or she performs. Thus in their nightly prostration, with the Power of the Reality of Intercession, saints intercede for their followers seeking not only forgiveness for their misdeeds, but also interceding in order that their good deeds and worship will be purified, "perfumed" and presented to the spiritual presence of the Prophet ﷺ. At that time—having been adorned by the spiritual power of the shaykh—the follower's deeds and worship become acceptable in the Divine Presence.

One of the great saints, Khwaja 'Ubaydullah al-Ahrar ق, had a follower who reached such a level. He passed the ten steps and so had become more than a lover (*muhib*), more than a beginner on the Path (*mubtadi'*) and more than one of the prepared ones (*musta'id*). The first three powers had already been opened to him. He was experiencing the Reality of Intercession, and in that reality he saw that his shaykh was written among the people of Hellfire. He was amazed. He thought, "It might be that he is doing something wrong that I do not know."

How could Hellfire be written for your shaykh? At the first opportunity, Satan comes to the mind. Because of this, the disciple may see something done by the shaykh and think that it is a blameworthy innovation. If you do not understand something the shaykh does, admit to yourself that you are not yet in a position to

---

[245] Bukhari.

understand, for Satan is always digging in our minds to bring out a bad smell.

That disciple saw on the Preserved Tablet (*Lawh al-Mahfoudh*) that his beloved shaykh was destined for Hellfire. So the disciple went into prostration every night and every day, praying, "O my Lord, take him from Hellfire and take him to Paradise." After one year, he raised his head one day and saw that his shaykh's name was taken from Hellfire to Paradise. He was very happy to have achieved his goal, and went to his shaykh to tell him the good news. Look at his arrogance! He went to the door of the shaykh, and all the disciples were there, sitting with discipline, majestic. Today we do not sit like that, since we are pampered babies. As soon as he entered, the shaykh—sitting with majesty—looked at him and said, "If you do not go back and return my name to where it was before, I will break you in half and you will no longer be my follower. Do not return until you change it back." He saw his sickness. The disciple, when given a little miraculous power, imagined himself to be higher than the shaykh.

For one year he made prostration in the morning and in the evening. It took him one year to bring his shaykh's name back to Hellfire, and he was so happy to see it there. He went back to the shaykh who was sitting with his disciples, and they were all in perfect discipline, unlike today. The shaykh told him, "Twenty-five years ago I reached the level you reached today, and I saw my name in Hellfire. I saw my name there, but I keep worshipping. Hell is Paradise for me if He wants to put me there. Every movement is by His Will. Training disciples for twenty-five years, I have seen it there and I never asked for it to be changed, although I am able to do so."

Bayazid al-Bistami ق asked God to put him in Hell with a body large enough to fill it all, and his request was accepted. He wanted to sacrifice himself for the good of all humanity occupying all of Hell and blocking anyone else from entering. With their love for all creation, God's saints may use the Reality of Intercession to save people from difficulties and punishment.

## 5. THE REALITY OF SCROLLING
## (*HAQIQATU 'T-TAYY*)

### SCROLLING THE DIMENSIONS OF SPACE

*The Day that We roll up the heavens like a scroll rolled
up for books (completed),- even as We produced the first
creation, so shall We produce a new one: a promise We
have undertaken: truly shall We fulfill it.*[246]

The reality of *tayy*, literally "to roll up" and reduce, is a jewel.
When it is given, it is an ornament that enables disciples to scroll
all over the world by means of the sacred formula, "In the name of
God, most Beneficent, most Munificent" (*bismillahi 'r-rahmani 'r-
rahim*). When disciples receive that jewel, they can move as they
like in the dimensions of space. Because they suffered so much,
God is generous with them. The spirit becomes free from the cage
of the body. The bodily cage is heavy, pulled by gravity; the spirit
is light, because it is heavenly. With that jewel, the soul is
liberated, and the body is put inside the spirit.[247] Then, like a
rocket, the spirit can transport the body.

The spirit moves faster than the speed of light. Light moves at
300,000 kilometers per second. When the use of thought (*tafkir*,
*muraqabah*) is purified, with nothing to disrupt it, it moves at a

---

[246] Suratu 'l-Anbiya [The Prophets], 21:104.
[247] This process recalls the mystical formula in Sufism, "Our spirits have become
our bodies and our bodies have become our spirits."

greater speed. The mind can reach the sun in one second. The speed of the heart is faster still; the way to move through the heart is far stronger. Energy can move anything. A small engine can lift the heaviest loads. Now vehicles use fuels relating to the earth that are transformed by their seclusion deep underground. The spirit is related to heavens. God knows what that energy is.

Why do we look at the power of the spirit as non-functional? You can make use of it, by using the power developed by saints. When they travel, the spirit contains the body until they arrive, and the body emerges. We can accept this process with an airplane, even though centuries ago it would not have seemed possible. To accept this spiritual process requires a foundation of belief in the Unseen.

Using the energy of the spirit, a person may be at home and may move at the same time to Makkah. Witnesses may report their presence in Makkah, though they can respond, "No, I was here in the house." Others may say, "You were in India." High-level saints are able to be in 12,000 places at one time. Low-level saints can move and appear in two or three places at the same time.

When saints move through Oceans of knowledge, they also move their followers. Wild geese migrate in flocks, and they move for months, from one continent to another. So the shaykh will move, moving his disciples with him in flocks. He cannot leave his disciples behind when he approaches the presence of the Prophet. If he did, the Prophet ﷺ would say, "Where are your disciples? I gave to you for the sake of those following you." The saint without his people is not a saint. Who is the Prophet ﷺ without his Community? A person must bring his flock with him, for the Prophet ﷺ said:

> *Each of you is a shepherd, and each one is responsible for his flock: The leader is shepherd of his nation and accountable for them; the man is shepherd of the family of his house and accountable for them; the servant is responsible for the wealth of*

*his master and accountable for it; and the woman is shepherd for the home of her husband and accountable for it.*[248]

For the Prophet ﷺ, not only is his Community coming for Intercession, but all prophets from Adam ﷺ go to him also. Every human being belongs to his Community.

The Reality of Scrolling moves mountains in space. Do not doubt it. With the space shuttle, some 2,500 tons of metal are going up and moving in space. If this is by the power of ordinary people, what about the power of the Friends of God? To them belongs the reality of scrolling universes, universes of knowledge.

God's first order to Prophet Muhammad ﷺ was *"Read!"*[249] The Prophet ﷺ asked, "What am I going to read?" *Iqra,* "read," can here be understood as "read these vibrations." *"Read in the name of your Lord who created,"*[250] means, "I created that from the Ocean of Power, *Bahr al-Qudrah.* Read that, O Muhammad. I am giving you the secret way to read creation. Read it and learn it. I am giving you that permission. I am giving you a language that encompasses all languages." That is why the Prophet ﷺ could hear the angel Gabriel when he revealed the Qur'an to him. What Gabriel gave to the Prophet ﷺ, no one knows. What God gave to Gabriel, no one knows.

This earth is a small planet in this universe, yet it is emitting frequencies. Similarly, the sun is emitting frequencies. Scientists say that there are 80 billion stars in our galaxy alone, and that there are six billion galaxies in this universe. All of them are emitting different frequencies and vibrations. However, as God said in the Holy Qur'an, *"you cannot understand their praising."*[251]

As an example, suppose I tap on a microphone. That tapping creates a sound that has a wavelength and the wavelength moves

---

[248] *Musnad* Ahmad and a similar narration is related in Bukhari.
[249] Suratu 'l-ʿAlaq [The Clot], 96:1.
[250] *Ibid.*
[251] Suratu 'l-Isra [The Night Journey], 17:44.

throughout space, throughout the universe, and never dies. Physicists and engineers know this fact. If you have a receiver, you can pick up that wave. If you do not have one, you do not hear it.

We are hearing from billions of years, voices coming from the universe, because we have big receivers. We are hearing some things yet we are not able to hear others. If you have the right equipment, every voice could be heard because waves move around the entire universe.

When the Prophet Muhammad ﷺ recited from the Holy Qur'an, that recitation became a wave that is ever-living and does not end. This is true, even from the point-of-view of physics. So, if that voice is there, why can we not hear it? Because there is something wrong with our equipment.

*God and His angels send blessings on the Prophet.*[252]

They are praising the Prophet. Can you hear it? No. With what kind of sound are they praising? God said that everything is praising Him, but you cannot understand it. That means this praise is by means of voices, and voices means there is a language. There must be a language of praise then.

Computers also "speak" many different languages, yet they often need to communicate with each other. To facilitate this, programmers developed software that translates one computer language into another, allowing computers that speak different languages to communicate with each other.

If a computer needs to communicate, what about this universe? How can the countless elements of the universe contact and communicate with each other? There must be a "software" for this, not an earthly one, but a heavenly "software" that can understand all the different frequencies and vibrations that God has given every creation in order that they may understand and communicate.

---

[252] Suratu 'l-Ahzab [The Confederates], 33:56.

That is why the Prophet Muhammad ﷺ used to hear the praising of the mountains when he passed them. That means God gave the Prophet Muhammad ﷺ that "software." We know from the Qur'an that the mountains were praising in unison with the Prophet David ﷺ:

> ... it was Our power that made the hills and the birds
> celebrate Our praises with David.[253]

This means that God gave those who are eligible to receive such an understanding a very high level of intelligence. For intellectual powers we speak of "intelligence quotient," or IQ. In spirituality, we do not speak of an IQ in this sense, but rather a spiritual IQ, ma'rifatullah: gnosis, or consciousness of God. God gave some of His servants this understanding so that they could comprehend what was occurring around them and how the parts of the universe communicated with each other. That is why in a holy Prophetic Tradition, God says:

> My servant draws not near to Me with anything more loved by
> Me than the religious obligations I have enjoined upon him, and
> My servant continues to draw near to Me with supererogatory
> works so that I shall love him. When I love him I am his hearing
> with which he hears, his seeing with which he sees, his hand with
> which he strikes, his foot with which he walks. Were he to ask
> something of Me, I would surely give it to him...[254]

"I will be the hearing with which he hears," means, "I will give him 'software' by which he can understand what cannot be understood by others, that will allow him to see what cannot be seen." He will be able to discern different frequencies, not just ultraviolet or infrared, but other frequencies that scientists do not know about. God will grant him sight and power by which he can see and hear these things. It means, "I will give him a special receiver to hear, by which he will hear what only a saint can

---

[253] Suratu 'l-Anbiya [The Prophets], 21:79.
[254] Bukhari.

hear." He will hear the voice that people cannot hear because they do not have that opening in their ears. God will give him from His Divine Attribute the Hearer, *as-Sam'i*, as Sariyya ☙ heard Sayyidina 'Umar's ☙ voice from Sham.

> *Ibn 'Umar ☙ said that his father, Sayyidina 'Umar ☙, was delivering a sermon on Friday. In the middle of his sermon, he shouted, "Ya Sariyya, al-jabal! O Sariyya! [look towards] the mountain!" Then he resumed his sermon and said, "He who stole a wolf, he oppressed," which means, "He who fed and watered the enemy, he committed an act of oppression."*
>
> *Some people looked at each other in dismay. Sayyidina 'Ali ☙ said to them, "He will likely say (something) about this statement."*
>
> *When the people had finished the prayer, they asked Sayyidina 'Umar ☙ about the incident. He said, "The idea crossed my mind that the enemy aggressors had defeated our brethren and they would run towards the mountain. Thus, if the Muslims moved towards the mountain, they would have to fight on one side only, while if they advanced, they would be destroyed. So those words escaped my mouth."*
>
> *After a month, a messenger came with good news. He said, "The people of the army heard Sayyidina 'Umar's ☙ voice on that day. We all went towards the mountain and God made us victorious."*[xxi]

That miracle (*karama*) was a sign that Sayyidina 'Umar ☙ had two characteristics from true faith: The Reality of Hearing, *'Ilmu 'l-Yaqin* and the Reality of Seeing, *'Aynu 'l-Yaqin*. The first characteristic is like one who has an audio tape. But when you have a video that is stronger—that brings you to the Reality of Certainty, *Haqqu 'l-Yaqin*. Sariyya ☙ and his troops were only able to hear from afar. They could not see Sayyidina 'Umar ☙, whereas Sayyidina 'Umar ☙ was seeing, hearing and speaking across the vast distance from Madina to Sham.

These people obeyed God and obeyed the Prophet. They truly followed the Sunnah. That "technology" is from 1,400 years ago, the time of the Prophet ﷺ. This power is based on the Prophetic Tradition in which God says, *"I will be the vision with which he sees."* If you are granted this power, you can see the Prophet. You can see how he is moving, how he is speaking, how he is acting and then you can follow his example. If you cannot do that, then follow those who can. Not everyone can do that, only a few Saints of God can do that, like Sayyidina 'Abd al-Qadir Jilani ق.

Mawlana Shaykh Nazim ق says that whoever keeps to true spiritual exercises, if he can complete them, there may appear from himself many forms like himself. First, there may be three, then seven, each having the same shape and bodily powers, but each one able to be in a different place. Each one is independent, looking, acting and knowing. This power comes from completing the aforementioned spiritual exercises under the supervision of a Perfect Master (*Murshidun Kamil*).

Mawlana Shaykh Nazim ق relates:

Bayazid ق once prayed one Friday congregational prayer in 24,000 different places. He told the religious authorities in one place: "I was praying in 12,000 different houses of worship today."

They asked, "How?"

He said, "By the power of the Lord Almighty. If you do not believe me, send people around to ask."

They sat and waited until messengers returned, saying that he was seen in so many places. Bayazid ق later said, "I was afraid to say 24,000, so I only said 12,000."

God says that, when one plants a single grain of wheat, it disappears into the earth and becomes seven ears, each ear with a hundred grains, 700 grains coming from one. If a person gives his body up, accepting to be nothing, God will grant him a body from His Divine Presence. Do not be surprised about God's actions; He is al-Qadir, The All-Powerful. But no one agrees to be nothing. Everyone is asking to be something, to be, to be, to be, even in religion.

In the Sufi way, too, people desire miracles and heavenly visions. No one likes to be nothing. When agreeing to be nothing, you will be all things. The Palace of Unity is not open to those saying, "We are something." You must enter into *khalwah*, seclusion, not thinking to come out finished, addressing to your ego and saying, "Don't think that you are coming out able to do miracles. I am going to bury you. My shaykh will send the Angel of Death to take your soul." Then it will be real seclusion. Otherwise, it is only training. For the first condition, the shaykh looks to the disciple to see if desires of the ego are still running in his heart. Ego must be finished there. Then such a person ready for death and all keys to treasures can be entrusted to him.

This body must be taken. Everyone will die. Some may offer themselves to death with their willpower. This does not mean killing oneself, but killing the ego's desires. Then you are ready for Divine powers.

Let us take the example of magic. There are stage magicians who pull rabbits out of their top hats and use sleight of hand and optical illusions to fool people. But there are also real magicians, who use real magic. Did you not hear that God said in Holy Qur'an that he sent two angels teaching people magic? What is that magic; how does it work?

First of all, it must be understood that everything has a frequency or wavelength. Depending on its frequency, it is either visible or invisible. When you change that frequency, it disappears. That is what magicians do. They can change the frequency of an object to make it appear or disappear at will.

> *Moses said, "Throw ye (first)." So when they threw,*
> *they bewitched the eyes of the people, and struck terror*
> *into them: for they showed a great (feat of) magic.*[255]

---

[255] Suratu 'l-'Araf [The Heights], 7:116.

If a magician can do that, what about the Friends of God? Can they not do more than that? Certainly, God will give a pious, sincere servant who devoted his life to God and the Prophet ﷺ even more wondrous powers.

Physicists say that sunlight is composed of seven primary colors. In reality, however, there are more than seven colors. You might be able to identify twenty colors or at most thirty, but sunlight consists of an infinite number of colors.

Every night Saints of God sit in the association called the Circle of Saints (*Diwan al-awliya*) in the presence of the Prophet Muhammad's soul and the souls of all the other prophets and messengers. There are hierarchies among the Saints of God that we do not perceive. God gave this nation inheritors of the prophets. God sent 124,000 prophets, and each Prophet ﷺ has an inheritor. Therefore, there are 124,000 saints in every time. When one passes away, another takes his place.

The number of prophets, 124,000, was told to us by the Prophet's cousin, Ibn 'Abbas ﷺ, who was known as the greatest commentator of Qur'an.

> *When Moses came to the place appointed by Us, and his Lord addressed him, He said: "O my Lord! show (Thyself) to me, that I may look upon thee."*[256]

The Prophet Moses ﷺ thought he was so close to God, for he is known in the Divine Presence as *Kalimullah*—the one who speaks with God. He was in full concentration and meditation, and in that state he was able to hear the heavenly voice[257], to hear God.

> *He said: "O my Lord! show (Thyself) to me, that I may look upon thee." God said: "By no means canst thou see Me (direct); But look upon the mount; if it abide in its place, then shalt thou see Me."* [258]

---

[256] Suratu 'l-'Araf, 7:143.
[257] Arabic: *hatif rabbani*.
[258] Suratu 'l-'Araf [The Heights], 7:143.

It means, "O Moses! If you want to come to Me you must look at that mountain." Ibn al-'Arabi ق said in *Futuhat al-Makkiyya*, that the mountain represents Prophet Moses' ﷺ ego, meaning no one can come to God's Presence with his ego. For that reason, God first sent Prophet Moses ﷺ and his servant and successor, Joshua ﷺ, to Sayyidina Khidr ﷺ to learn a specialized knowledge that even he, as one of the five greatest prophets, did not know.

> *So they found one of Our servants, on whom We had*
> *bestowed Mercy from Ourselves and whom We had*
> *taught knowledge from Our own Presence.*[259]

He said, "Come to Me by throwing away the self. Look at the mountain, if it remains in its place then you will see Me."

> *When his Lord manifested His glory on the Mount, He*
> *made it as dust. And Moses fell down in a swoon. When*
> *he recovered his senses he said: "Glory be to Thee! To*
> *Thee I turn in repentance, and I am the first to*
> *believe."*[260]

In explaining that verse, Ibn 'Abbas ﷺ said, "When he awoke, that mountain disappeared and in its place before him was a huge mountain made up of 124,000 prophets."[261]

The prophets have inheritors in every era who are living shaykhs. They can say to a mountain, "Move!" and it will move. They may appear as an attraction, like a spotlight in a stadium, a beacon or a rainbow. When people see them, they fall into states of ecstasy.

When the Saints of God say, "We are seeing this," you cannot say, "No." They are seeing frequencies that your eye cannot.

After Prophet Muhammad ﷺ went on the Night Journey and Ascension, he returned and saw everything that had passed took

---

[259] Suratu 'l-Kahf [The Cave] 18:65.
[260] Suratu 'l-Kahf, 18:65.
[261] Isma'eel Haqqi's *Ruh al-Bayan*.

place in the blink of an eye. He went with body and soul, yet when he came back, his bed was still warm.

Imam Sha'rawi related that Imam Nawawi said, "The Prophet ☆ saw his Lord with the eyes of his head."[262] God raised him up with a body that could discern the frequencies that fill this universe. These vibrations or signs can be known, but you need to have the software. If you can establish that software in your heart then you can see what others cannot see.

Consider what God says about the Prophet Solomon ☆:

> *He said (to his own men): "Ye chiefs! which of you can*
> *bring me her throne before they come to me in*
> *submission?" Said an 'Ifrit, of the Jinns: "I will bring it*
> *to thee before thou rise from thy council: indeed I have*
> *full strength for the purpose, and may be trusted."* [263]

The Jinn said, "I can bring the Throne of Sheba, but not immediately. I need time, and by then your meeting will be ending."

> *Said one who had knowledge of the Book: "I will bring it*
> *to thee within the twinkling of an eye!" Then when*
> *(Solomon) saw it placed firmly before him, he said: "This*
> *is by the Grace of my Lord!"* [264]

The one "who had knowledge of the book"[xxii] said, "I will bring it to you in the blink of an eye." He brought it there using his knowledge of these frequencies. The Throne of Sheba appeared in front of their eyes. He used a power similar to that of satellite television today.

Today many people speak of the need for a path to transformation. The saints of God are themselves a path to transformation. They are those who dedicated their lives to love of God, love of Prophet ☆, love of faith. They know the path to

---

[262] Arabic: *ra' rabbihi bi 'aynay rasih.*

[263] Suratu 'n-Naml [The Ant], 27:38-39.

[264] Suratu 'n-Naml, 27:40.

transformation. If one is in the East, they can bring him to the West, and if one is in the East they can bring him to the West in order to be seen.

Our master Shaykh Nazim ق says:

To fly through this space is so easy; with the blink of an eye a person can reach Heavens which physically would take billions of years. Our light is not like the one coming from the sun; our light belongs to the Oceans of Divine Lights, that is why the speed of our soul is so fast. It is like comparing a person riding on a donkey to someone sitting in a rocket. That is an analogy to the difference between the speed of light and the speed of our Divine Lights.

If you want a proof then go out and look, how long does it take you to see the furthest galaxy? The moment you look, your eyes are there! The galaxy of Andromeda is millions of light years away but with the naked eye it is a small spot which you can see. They say there are 300 millions of stars but for us it looks like a tiny spot within the greatness of space. That is part of your soul power, just a small part of it. If the whole power of your soul was on, you could see the whole universe in its real existence! You wouldn't just see Andromeda like a spot, you would see the huge galaxy in its greatness. It means you will see every one of the 300 millions of stars in it. Today, even with the Hubble telescope, one can see the stars of Andromeda—what then is the power of the soul? Divine Lights are Lights from God. But it is closed off now because our physical desires prevent it. We are only interested in what we are eating, drinking, or enjoyment, nothing else. We are just wasting our huge powers.

Now most people are nearly under the command of their ego; therefore the entire world is out of control. On the other hand, if people control their ego with their will power then they will be free from the gravity of their self.

231

At that time they can travel all around the universe and even beyond!

We, mankind, have souls and soul desires to be in Heaven; it is not interested in eating, drinking, or physical enjoyment. Such desires belong to our physical being, and they are endless. That is why we get hungry and thirsty physically. If we do not control these desires, they will be the biggest problem. Try to control them. We cannot live without them, but if we do not control them, they will be the greatest destruction. Prophet Muhammad ﷺ said:

*Whoever guarantees for me what is between his jaws and what is between his legs, I will guarantee him Paradise.*[265]

Mankind needs a balance for its desires, to learn how to control them. For example if you give me a car I would not know how to control it, because I have never been trained to. It is not easy, but you can learn, and then it is simple. The ego is the strongest force in existence and it needs to be controlled. A car or an airplane which is out of control, it cannot be saved by anything! Our ego is much more complicated and powerful than an aircraft.

If anyone wants to learn to drive a vehicle there are lots of schools for doing so. But what about the ego? You think you can do that yourself? No! If it had been the case it would not have been necessary to have sent all those prophets, and after them saints. Holy people are able to control themselves; they teach people how to do that, how to keep their physical desires in limits. If you can control that huge power you may fly, and rise to Heavens without wings, just with your will power, you can go anywhere, even beyond this universe. Heaven doesn't belong to this world; the souls of human beings were made from Divine Lights.

---

[265] Bukhari.

In late 1980s, the prime minister and the mayor of Beirut invited Mawlana Shaykh Nazim ق to go with them on Pilgrimage to Makkah, Hajj. He did not say yes or no, but said, "I will see."

The prime minister insisted. Again, Mawlana did not say, "No," nor did he say, "Yes." He kept his answer vague.

We spent the rest of the month with Mawlana, in Tripoli, and the celebration of the Eid of the Sacrifice came and went. Then the pilgrims began to return from Hajj. The next day, we went to see the mayor and the prime minister to congratulate them on completing the Pilgrimage. Disgruntled, they looked at Mawlana Shaykh Nazim ق. They said, "Mawlana Shaykh Nazim, we invited you to come with us, but you did not come with us and instead went with someone else."

We were young, so we were troublemakers. We asked them, "Why are you saying this?" They said, "We met Mawlana Shaykh Nazim at the Ka'ba, during the circumambulation, *tawaf*.[266] He did the circumambulation with us there, and when he finished the circling, he left and we left."

Mawlana Shaykh Nazim ق never left Lebanon. He was in our home for the entire time of the Pilgrimage. That is how the Saints of God move in space. They transform their frequencies and appear at another place.

## SCROLLING IN THE DIMENSION OF TIME

The shaykh holds the power to give his followers true dreams. Many people come to me and say, "I saw a shaykh in my dream. He looked like this and gave me this to recite." Later, they encounter the shaykh physically and realize that he was the one they met in the dream. A guide can reach anyone in the world through dreams and visions. People can become devoted followers and even take orders from the shaykh through dreams and visions. He has that power.

---

[266] Circumambulation of the Ka'ba, done seven times.

The guide gives his follower awareness (*yaqaza*), so that they will not be heedless. Then he breathes with the awareness that, at any moment, God can stop him from inhaling or exhaling. This means that, in every moment, with the guide's grace that he takes from the Prophet Muhammad ﷺ, the follower will be remembering his Lord though his breath.

For many of us, breathing is something the body does automatically. When you are talking, you might be unaware that you are breathing in and out, but dive into the sea and you will remember your breathing. A Purifying Shaykh (*shaykhu 't-tazkiyya*) makes you aware that, at every moment, you are submerged in an ocean, that the energy you take in or put out belongs to God's Power.

There is a *dhikr* for when you exhale and when you inhale, and Divine Names to recite depending upon the time and conditions of the day. Each inhalation and each exhalation belongs to a Name of God. There are ten angels accompanying each inhalation, and ten angels accompanying each exhalation. Each angel is created from a different light belonging to God. Grandshaykh 'Abd Allah ق said that nine parts of each light is from Sayyidina Muhammad ﷺ and one is from the Ocean of Power. These lights are not the Light of God. We are servants to God and cannot share His Light. The Saints of God say that human beings take 24,000 breaths in 24 hours. Only a Purifying Shaykh can put on your tongue the remembrance of God with every breath. In reality, every breath is remembrance, but you are heedless of it.

Once you reach the awareness of the 24,000 breaths, awareness is increased to the level of 700,000 per day. At this stage, time is extended in order to allow you to call upon your Lord 700,000 times. Time is unrolled without making it longer, just as God can make the entire world pass through the eye of a needle without making the world smaller or the needle larger.[xxiii] This is a power of the tongue (*ta'i al-lisan*), and it is from the Reality of Scrolling. It is the ability to recite more by using the energy of the spirit.

How is this possible? God created a vein under the tongue that reaches directly to the heart. By following the guide, the disciple progresses and darkness is removed from the tongue and heart. At that time you become luminous (*nurani*), since you are no longer relying upon the body, or the tongue, but upon that heavenly light. Whatever is related to the Divine can do anything. The mind relates to the earth. When people become luminous, the following holy Prophetic Tradition applies to them, in which God says:

> *Neither the heavens nor earth contain Me, but the heart of my believing servant contains Me.*[xxiv]

That heart can do miracles, reaching seven million repetitions in *dhikr*, even 70 million. So much is granted to any human being who follows the Saints of God.

# حقيقة الارشاد

## 6. THE REALITY OF GUIDANCE
### (*HAQIQATU 'L-IRSHAD*)

*By His Grace God guided the believers to the Truth,
concerning that wherein they differed. For God guided
whom He will to a path that is straight.*[267]

When you are dressed with all these realities, you are given the
sixth power: the ability to guide people. Now you speak and it is
your ego speaking. People come and sit and listen to lecturers, but
only their egos are speaking. After you have been dressed with
these realities, you can guide someone to his or her eternal life.

Everyone has a different eternal life. Whatever God has
planned for the individual, the shaykh will guide him by the
hand, step by step, to move him forward. Someone in a maze who
is unable to find the door out is lost. Guidance will take you left,
right, right, left, then straight until you come out. Not everyone
knows how to get out of this maze. You need to have a guide in
order to escape. To get out of the tunnel, one must have all kinds
of lights in order to pass safely.

The Reality of Guidance is knowledge of spirituality. The saint
knows how to heal you from all kinds of worldly attachments,
and so take you up to heavenly attachments in order that you will
be able to penetrate through space to your final destination.

---

[267] Suratu 'l-Baqara [The Cow], 2:213.

236

On the Day of Promises, when God asked the assembled souls, "Am I not your Lord?" they answered, "Yes!" The shaykh guides you to that affirmation. You do not remember it now. God took from us a covenant, an oath. What you accepted on that day was recorded. One day it will be opened for you, what you accepted on the Day of Promises in the Presence of God. Until then, you have to fulfill your requirements, like a person studying to become a doctor. Thus, we follow guidance in order to fulfill what we promised our Lord.

> *"Lo! We offered the trust unto the heavens and the earth and the hills, but they shrank from bearing it and were afraid of it. And man assumed it. Lo! he hath proved a tyrant and a fool."* [268]

The heavens and earth and mountains did not accept, but because of his ignorance, man has become an oppressor to himself.

When you climb up to reach the Reality of Guidance, you can see what kind of oath you took. That will be your journey to your reality. Then they will dress you with guidance, and give you permission. Until then, you are like a toy that speaks, like a parrot, as are today's scholars and lecturers. That is not guidance. Guidance is only for the saints of God.

There are really seven powers hidden within the human being, but this explanation of these realities is enough.

---

[268] Suratu 'l-Ahzab [The Confederates], 33:72.

# ENDNOTES

i About the wording, "My Lord came to me in the best image (*surah*)," Mullah Ali al-Qari observed, "God is exalted from possessing a body, a form (*surah*), and directions with regard to His essence," when he wrote about this Prophetic Tradition in the chapter on the Prophet's ﷺ turban in his book *Jam al-wasa'il fi sharh al-shama'il*, a commentary on Tirmidhi's *Shama'il* or *Characteristics of the Prophet* ﷺ. He also said:

> Whether the Prophet ﷺ saw his Lord during his sleep or whether Allah the Glorious and Exalted manifested Himself to him with a form (*bi al-tajalli al-suwari*), this type of manifestation is known among the masters of spiritual states and stations (*arbab al-hal wa al-maqam*), and it consists in being reminded of His qualities (*hayatihi*) and reflecting upon His vision (*ruyatihi*), which is the outcome of the perfection of one's inner detachment (*takhliyatihi*) and self-adornment (*tahliyatihi*).

ii A version similar to this is related in *Lore of Light*, Vol. 1, Hajjah Amina Hattun, and yet another version is related by as-Sufuri in *Nuzhat al-Majalis* as:

> When God created the Pen, He said, "Write My Oneness: 'There is no god except God.'" Then He said: "Write, 'Muhammad is the Messenger of God.'"
>
> When the Pen heard the name "Muhammad," it prostrated and said in its prostration, "Glory to the One Who is characterized with generosity; Glory be to the Gracious, the Most Compassionate. I have known your Greatest Name, so who is this Muhammad whose name You have joined with Yours?" Then God said, "Keep good manners O Pen! For by My Glory and My Majesty, I did not create My creation except for the love of Muhammad ﷺ." The Pen then split due to the sweetness of Muhammad ﷺ and said, "Peace be upon you, O Messenger of God." But it found no one to respond to its greeting, upon which

238

God said, "And peace be unto you, and My mercy and My blessings."

iii The first part is a Prophetic Tradition, but the second, while often attributed to the Prophet ﷺ is in fact as as-Sakhawi noted in his *Maqasid*, "not attributed to the Prophet ﷺ, rather it is the words of Harith bin Kaldah, a physician of the Arabs or from someone else." Al-Hafiz as-Suyuti said the same in his *al-Hawi* and his own commentary of the Prophetic Traditions he used in his exegesis *ad-Durar*, attributed it to a *Tabi'* or a *hakim* (physician) or an Israelite tradition and he added at the end of the saying, "and the head of every fault is the love of the world." Ibn 'Arabi mentioned it in his *Futuhat*, Ibn 'Ata-Allah in his *Hikam*.

iv As-Sufuri in *Nuzhat al-majalis*. Another version is: "Contemplation for one hour on the alteration of the night and day is better than eighty years of worship," (ad-Daylamī). Yet another version is related: "Contemplation for one hour is better than sixty years of worship," (Abu ash-Shaykh in his *Azamah*).

v Al-Ajlouni says, "Al-Ghazali mentioned it in *Ihya 'ulum ad-din*." Al-Sakhawi said in *al-Maqasid*, following his shaykh al-Suyuti in *al-La'ali*, "There is no known chain from the Prophet ﷺ for it, and its meaning is that his heart can contain belief in Me, love of Me and gnosis of Me." And it is similar to the Israelite tradition Ahmad has related in *al-Zuhd* from Wahb bin Munabbih who said that God opened the heavens for Ezekiel until he saw the Throne, so Ezekiel said, 'How Perfect are You! How Mighty are You, O Lord!' So God said, 'Truly, the heavens and the earth were too weak to contain Me, but the soft, humble heart of My believing slave contains Me.'"

vi "This place is called Magharat al-dam, the Cave of Blood, on Mt. Qasiyun, above today's Damascus. And the blood ran downhill onto the stone where it congealed and remains to this day, because the earth refused to absorb this blood. It can be seen there today, as a sign of the first crime on earth."
Hajjah Amina Adil, *Lore of Light*, Volume 1, Arafat Publishing, Sri Lanka, 1989, p. 36.

vii Located at the Station of the Forty, Maqam al-Arba'in, is a mosque containing forty prayer niches, one for each of the special saints of Greater Syria (Sham), known as the Abdal or Budala.

'Ali ibn Abi Talib ⚘ said, "...I heard the Messenger of God ﷺ say, 'The Substitutes (*al-abdal*) are in Syria and they are forty men, every time one of them dies, God substitutes another in his place. By means of them God brings down the rain...." (*Musnad* Ahmad).

A number of other narrations on this topic are cited in *The Approach of Armageddon? An Islamic Perspective*, Shaykh Muhammad Hisham Kabbani, Islamic Supreme Council of America, 2003, in the chapter "Sham and the Abdal."

viii The Prophet ﷺ said, "There is none among you in whom there is not a devil." They said, "Even in you, O Messenger of God?" He said, "Even in me, but God helped me to overcome him and he has submitted to me, so he doesn't order anything except good." *Sahih Muslim*.

ix From a hadith narrated by al-Hakim in his *Mustadrak*, ibn Hibban in his *Sahih*, at-Tabarani in his *al-Kabir* and al-Bazzar. In a similar Tradition, the Prophet ﷺ said "Whoever says *La ilaha illa-Allah*, it will be his salvation someday, no matter what befalls him before that." (Bayhaqi). Another Tradition related by Abu Dharr ⚘ who said, the Prophet ﷺ said, "Whoever says 'There is no god but God,' enters Paradise even if he commits adultery and even if he steals." (Nasa'i, at-Tabarani and others, *sahih*) And in yet another Tradition, the Prophet ﷺ said, "No-one ever witnesses that there is no god but God and that I am God's Messenger and then enters the Fire nor is consumed by it." Anas said, "This hadith impressed me so much that I ordered my son to write it down and he did," (Muslim). There are many other Traditions of similar import.

x Eve bore Adam ﷺ their first children Cain and his twin sister, while in the Garden. When Adam ﷺ and Eve were cast out of the Garden, she bore Abel and his twin sister. According to the biographer of the Prophet ﷺ, Ibn Ishaq:

> When they grew up, Adam ﷺ commanded his son Cain to marry the twin of Abel and he ordered Abel to marry the twin of Cain. Abel agreed to that and was pleased, but Cain refused... Cain's sister was one of the most beautiful people, and Cain begrudged her to his brother and wanted her for himself... His father said to him, "O my son, she is not licit for you." But Cain refused to accept that on his father's authority, so his father said to him, "O my son, offer a sacrifice, and your brother Abel will offer a sacrifice. Which of the two sacrifices God accepts, he has the

greater right to her." Cain was a sower of the earth and Abel a tender of flocks; Cain offered wheat, and Abel offered the firstlings of his sheep and goat, and some say he even sacrificed a cow. God, the Mighty and the Powerful, sent a white fire which consumed Abel's sacrifice, leaving the sacrifice of Cain. That was how God, the Almighty and the Powerful, accepted sacrifices. When God accepted Abel's sacrifice, judging in his favor about Cain's sister, Cain became angry. Pride vanquished him and the Devil urged him on. So he followed his brother Abel while he was walking about and killed him.

Ibn Ishaq, *The Making of the Last Prophet* (Sirah Ibn Ishaq), reconstructed by Gordon D. Newby, University of South Carolina Press, 1989, p. 38-40.

xi The Prophet ﷺ said, "I do not fear that you will become polytheists after me, but I fear that, because of worldly interests, you will fight each others, and thus be destroyed like the peoples of old." Bukhari and Muslim.

xii These two times are related through the Time Dilation formula:

$$t' = t/(\sqrt{1 - v^2/c^2})$$

Here, we have:

- $t'$ is the time of the stationary frame, so it is the normal time of worship (70 years)
- $t$ is the time of the moving frame, so it is the time of meditation (1 hour)

Then, the only unknown is $v$, the speed of the traveling soul. We may therefore solve for this $v$, and the result will give us the minimum speed at which one must move in order to gain 70 years of worship through 1 hour of meditation according to our beloved Prophet ﷺ. So using the numbers given by Prophet Muhammad ﷺ, we came up with a minimum value for the speed of the soul in *muraqabah*, and this value is extremely close to $c$, the Muhammadan Light, exactly as Einstein's Special Theory of Relativity predicted. Mathematically speaking, this result implies that in order to gain 70 years of worship through 1 hour of *muraqabah*, one needs to travel at least at 99.9999999999% the speed of Light. Spiritually speaking, this is a proof that reaching the speed of Light will "unlock" the door of Eternity, which is the Kingdom in which dwells the Presence of the Light of Prophet ﷺ.

The mathematical result we found may be summarized as follows: when a soul is doing *muraqabah*, it is approaching the Light of Prophet ﷺ, and this process is manifested in science as the value of the soul's traveling speed that approaches the value of the speed of Light, **c**.

xiii All of Sayyidina Bayazid's ق suffering was because he made one controversial statement that caused everyone to oppose him. Sometimes saints want to check who is with them and who is against, so they throw out a controversial issue and watch the hearts of those present. Those who remain 'with' the saint will be raised, and he will pray and ask forgiveness for those who curse and speak against him "because they mentioned my name." That is the wisdom of making controversial statements. The controversial statement that he made was that he said, "Everyone bow to me," although in saying this he did not ask for them to bow to him, but rather to the Divine Light within him. That was enough to take him to prison.

Similarly, the great saint Ibn 'Arabi ق was accused of polytheism and unbelief and killed when he said "What you worship is under my feet." Many years later the Ottoman Sultan Sulayman excavated that site and found a huge treasure trove of gold. The true import of Ibn 'Arabi's ق statement was 'You people are too engrossed in money and materialism, making it more important than God Almighty.' Rather than denying God and committing open polytheism, he was pointing out the materialistic hidden polytheism of the people

xiv This narration has no basis, but a *hadith* with similar purport is found in Ibn Majah, "Verily to God belong receptacles from the people of the earth; and the receptacles of your Lord are the hearts of His sincere servants, and the most beloved of them to him are the most lenient and the most soft."

xv Shaykh Shamsuddin Habibullah Jan-i-Janan al-Mazhar ق (1701-1781), the twenty-ninth master of the Naqshbandi lineage, was a successor in India of the Mujaddadi lineage traced to Ahmad al-Faruqi, the twenty-fifth master, and is one of the Golden Chain of masters.

xvi To bring your heart back to its original purity the spiritual guide will "reformat your hard drive." The data of old sins will be purged, but in the process these will come across the screen of your consciousness. In order not to be bogged down by these negative images from the past, the student must keep reciting, "I seek God's forgiveness (*astaghfirullah*)" for as long as the sinister thoughts remain.

xvii Muslim narrated it. The last portion is:

> The man said, "Now tell me about the Hour." The Prophet replied, "The one who is being asked knows no more about it than the questioner." He said, "Then tell me about its signs." He replied, "The slave-girl will give birth to her mistress, and you will see the barefoot, naked, destitute herdsmen outdo each other in erecting tall buildings." Then he left and time passed. Later he said to me, "O 'Umar, do you know who that was asking questions?" I said, "God and His Messenger know best." He said, "He was none other than Gabriel. He came to you to teach you your religion."

xviii In Divine Law, *Shari'ah*, this prostration (*sajda*) is not the prostration of worship, but is called *sajdat al-ihtiram*, the prostration of respect. Prior to the advent of Prophet Muhammad ﷺ, it was a permitted action.

xix While suicide even in penitence is strictly prohibited in Islam, the spiritual import of this verse should not be overlooked. The order to "slay yourselves" applies to extinguishing the blameworthy traits and characteristics such that one becomes a perfected human being, achieving a state of perfect submission to God's will while still in this world. As Prophet Muhammad ﷺ said, "If anyone wants to see someone who has died before he died, he should look to Abu Bakr Siddiq."

xx "There are jewels in man which have influences on him. The jewel of awe and marvel, the finest of these jewels, is in the center of the human heart. It is where the essence of the being is hidden, a store of energy and power. In that dark hidden place many an unknown secret is kept...That spot in the center of the human being, in his heart, is...a black spot." (Ibn 'Arabi, *Divine Governance of the Human Kingdom*, translated by Shaikh Tosun Bayrak, Fons Vitae, 1997, page 180).

xxi It is reported from his son 'Abd Allah ؓ that his father Sayyidina 'Umar ؓ [who was caliph at the time] dispatched an army, designating one man named Sariyya ؓ leader (*amir*) over it. It is said that one day Sayyidina 'Umar ؓ was delivering the Friday sermon [in Madinah]. During the sermon he said loudly "*Ya Sariyya al-jabal!* O Sariyya! [towards] the mountain." Then [later] a courier came from the army and said, "O Commander of the Faithful! We were on the verge of being defeated when we heard a voice thrice: *'Ya Sariyya al-jabal!'* So we moved the back of our army near the mountain and Allah Most Holy defeated them." Ibn 'Umar ﷺ says that Sayyidina 'Umar ﷺ was told that it was he who was shouting in that voice.

It says in one tradition that the people said to Sayyidina 'Ali ﷺ, "Did not you hear Sayyidina 'Umar that while delivering the sermon from the pulpit he said, *'Ya Sariyya al-jabal!'*? Sayyidina 'Ali ﷺ said, "A thousand pities for you! Leave Sayyidina 'Umar ﷺ alone! Whenever he has entered anything, he has surely acquitted himself well."

Both narrations are in *Life of the Companions*, by Shaykh Zakariyya Kandhalvi.

xxii The "book" in the time of Solomon was the Psalms of David (Zabur). If such powers were for one who has knowledge of the Psalms, then what about one who has knowledge of the Qur'an?

xxiii A reference to the verse:

> To those who reject Our signs and treat them with arrogance, no
> opening will there be of the gates of heaven, nor will they enter the
> garden, until the camel can pass through the eye of the needle: Such is
> Our reward for those in sin. (Suratu 'l-'Araf [The Heights], 7:40)

xxiv Al-Ghazali mentioned it in his *Revival of the Religious Sciences*. It is similar to the Israelite tradition Ahmad has related in *al-Zuhd* from Wahb bin Munabbih who said that God opened the heavens for Ezekiel until he saw the Throne, so Ezekiel said, "How Perfect are You! How Mighty are You, O Lord!" So God said, "Truly, the heavens and the earth were too weak to contain Me, but the soft, humble heart of my believing slave contains Me."